Dollarizing Differentiation Value

Pierre Schaeffer, Chief Marketing Officer, Thales
Pricing based on customer value is a pillar of modern marketing. This book proposes practical and real-life actions that marketers can take to better segment their market, understand their differentiation, and design dollarized value propositions. A must-read!

Vishaal Jayaswal, Vice President of Client Solutions & Value Strategy, Cox Automotive Inc.
B2B companies have to be better at understanding their true differentiation and how to translate it into financial benefits for their customers. This book proposes a practical framework for extracting true differentiation and for dollarizing it. Reading it will change your views on how to draft your customer value propositions!

Kevin Lemke, Vice President of Pricing & Commercial Excellence, Stanley Black and Decker
Value-based pricing is much more than a pricing strategy—it is a go-to-market strategy. This book reinforces that reality and proposes a practical framework for managing value-based transformations. It covers the foundation of marketing: segmentation, differentiation, dollarization, and pricing. Stephan's energetic style and expert perspective shine throughout, making this book an engaging must-read for all commercially focused professionals.

Tom Wingren, Director of Pricing & Sales Development, Wartsila Marine Solutions
Dollarizing differentiation is the essence of value-based pricing. Liozu proposes concrete and practical guidelines for getting started and for using dollarization in go-to-market strategies. Reading this book will change the way you manage your customer value propositions across your entire organization!

Benoit Rengade, Business Process Owner, Value-based Pricing, Michelin
Everyone believes he does value selling, but is that really so? We keep falling into the same traps: thinking value in absolute terms, without reference to a next-best competitive offer; listing benefits but stopping short of putting a dollar tag on them; or, very often, believing value is the same for all customers. Stephan's book is all about avoiding the product-centric traps to really become customer-centric. And unlike most of its kind, it is easy to read and loaded with humor. A compelling read!

Dollarizing Differentiation Value

A Practical Guide for the Quantification and the Capture of Customer Value in B2B Markets

By Stephan M. Liozu, PhD

Value Innoruption Advisors Publishing • Sewickley PA • 2016

Dollarizing Differentiation Value
A Practical Guide for the Quantification and the Capture of Customer Value in B2B Markets
By Stephan M. Liozu, Ph.D.

Published by
Value Innoruption Advisors Publishing
PO Box 208
Sewickley, Pennsylvania 15143
www.valueinnoruption.com

EVE and Economic Value Estimation are registered trademarks of Monitor Company Group Limited Partnership. Stage-Gate is a registered trademark of Stage-Gate Inc. Figure 4.4. is adapted from material copyright 2003 MarketPlace LLC. Figure 6.1 is adapted from Macdivitt & Wilkinson, *Value-based Pricing*, McGraw Hill (2012). Figure 6.7 is adapted from Monitor Company Group Limited Partnership. Figure 6.18 screen shot courtesy of LeveragePoint Innovations. Trademarks shown in Figures 4.6 and 12.2 are the property of their respective owners.

ISBN: 978-1-945815-00-3 trade paperback
ISBN: 978-1-945815-01-0 ebook

Second printing

Design and composition: www.dmargulis.com

MANUFACTURED IN THE UNITED STATES OF AMERICA

To my loved ones!

Thank you for giving me your support and your love, and for helping me discover my own journey in life!

Contents

Acknowledgments

EXPERTISE IN CUSTOMER VALUE management does not come overnight. It comes with experience, exploration, and practice. The dollarization of differentiation value is both a science and an art. Theories in the field have to be tested, adapted, and mindfully assimilated. I am grateful for the support from many B2B companies who trusted me to guide them through value transformations and who allowed me to develop and refine the knowledge proposed in this book. I want to acknowledge the dozens of business leaders who have had the courage to transform their go-to-market approaches and have taken bold steps to become value masters as I define them here. These B2B leaders are pioneers in the field of dollarized value propositions and are the initiators of the value-based pricing revolution.

Dollarizing
Differentiation
Value

Introduction

THE SLOW PACE OF *global economic growth is causing an existential crisis in many firms, regardless of size and industry. They face an urgent question that sounds so deceptively simple:*

"What value *do we deliver to our customers versus our competitors?"*

Now is the time to answer that "value" question so well and so completely that your organization thrives. The biggest winners in the 21st century will have value-based strategies, value-based innovation, value-based marketing, and value-based pricing. There has never been a more exciting and lucrative time to pay attention to value and turn a daunting question of survival into a sustainable answer of success.

The question sounds deceptively simple, but you will discover quickly that this "value" question is tough to answer. Value seems hard to define, hard to measure, and hard to improve. At the same time, your clock is ticking. Commoditization is disrupting business models and forcing business-to-business (B2B) companies to re-evaluate their internal and external processes, especially their customer value propositions. Things are changing so fast. You may have a strong advantage today with pricing power, and it can evaporate in three months. You have to be faster than the market, and you have to be vigilant. This means a lot more formal, mindful management of value in all its aspects, from strategy to pricing.

This disruption has many sources. Demand patterns are going up and down within a narrow range, and growth in developed countries is less than half the annual rate of the previous strong growth periods in our lifetimes. The United States is holding its own, but Europe is soft. Emerging markets are going down, and China is slowing down. A comment in General Electric's 2000 annual report attributed to Jack Welch, the former CEO of GE, speaks for itself: "We've long believed that when the rate of change inside an institution becomes slower than the rate of change outside, the end is in sight. The only question is when." This leads to much greater competition as we all fight for the same pies. It is dangerous to try to win on price, because price wars only reduce the profit pool. The answer must come from business model innovation centered on value.

Commoditization is changing everything for B2B companies as they struggle with stagnation and battle with uncertainty: what they do, and how they spend their money, on innovation, product development, talent, and strategy. Companies are now acquiring demand instead of creating demand through superior products. Consolidation is the expedient way out, but it only buys some time before the same existential "value" question comes back.

Rising customer expectations began changing the game for B2B companies years ago, and the situation is intensifying. The combination of tenacious professional B2B buyers and ubiquitous 24/7 communications technology has made pricing very transparent. B2B buyers are more sophisticated, have access to better technology, and are well trained to break down weak value-based approaches and to dilute perceived differentiation. You need robust, rational ones.

Everything is online, information is no longer scarce, and there is no longer any place to hide. A commoditization mindset has taken hold. Price wars are prevalent. Price concessions are expected at every interaction. Further down the value chain, the situation is no different. Distribution channels are focused on short-term costs and can sometimes be a "value bottleneck." End users have access to more information and more choices. They want more every day and eagerly take advantage of greater price transparency.

This puts customer value propositions and prices under more scrutiny than ever in modern history. Literally. In this book I recommend that you fight transparency with transparency. You need to dollarize your relative value. This means quantifying the benefits you deliver in hard dollars and cents versus competition, and defending them with rational, evidence-based stories.

To do that, though, you need the most thorough understanding of value that you can get. With your core value models under attack, you can't wait for two years and hope that the economy turns around or the pressures go away. Hope is not a strategy. You have to rebuild your value propositions from the ground up.

Some industries have begun that transformation. They know that disruption also creates opportunities. Inflationary pressures have emerged in some specialty industries, where firms have gotten the message that you can't keep opening plants and adding capacity or buying up rivals. Chemicals is a good example. Many players have begun to manage with a focus on value, not volume. At a time when oil at $30 would dictate price cuts, these companies are raising prices or maintaining their pricing power by limiting capacity and constraining demand. They are changing the game. At the same time, they are showing that value transformations can happen.

This book will guide you to making *your* value transformation happen. It focuses on value-based approaches that traditionally begin with VBP and then spread to value-based innovation and value-based selling. So I will contextualize my overarching message about the need to pay attention to customer value and to quantify your differentiation value within the methods of VBP. I do this because my experience shows that most value transformations are launched because of severe pricing problems. While I agree that the symptom is pricing erosion, generally, the structural causes of the pricing problems are deeply rooted in a lack of innovation, a lack of understanding of customer value, a lack of segmentation, and a misconception of the concept of differentiation. Thus this book!

Motivations: Let's finally get a simple, practical, powerful definition of "value-based"

Everyone has heard it. Value-based anything, especially value-based pricing, has become a cliché. Consultants and academics like to throw the term around because it has a compelling aspirational quality. You can kind of define it, but no one does it—or does it well—because there has never been a practical blueprint for how to do it. Everyone else touches on it and has a part on economic value analysis, but no one has written that workhorse book on this essential topic, the book that offers simple, practical, realistic, and powerful clarity and guidance all at the same time. Until now!

Let's focus for now on value-based pricing (VBP). There are too many confusing definitions for VBP, and the pricing profession has not yet made a strong enough case for its widespread adoption. Marketing and pricing leaders understand the theory, but they do not know how to operationalize it in practical terms. They can cite the underlying ideas chapter and verse, but deep knowledge is only one part of the solution. For value-based initiatives to take hold and succeed over the long term, their sponsors need to dispel the myths, explain the benefits, and create excitement. These transformations are just like any other journey in life. If you want someone to join you on a trip, you show them snapshots and videos that bring the scenery and the attractions to life. You don't blind them with science, make PowerPoints, or read them pages from an encyclopedia.

VBP is much more than a pricing strategy, and it needs to be looked at as part of a holistic value transformation. That value transformation makes your life easier, saves your company money, and delights your customers—if you are willing to make the investment. As you read this book, you will come to see such a transformation as a desirable and achievable goal to pursue, not a scary obligation to evade.

I train and certify thousands of executives every year. This book distills the guidance they have received from me and some of the success stories they have achieved. Little has been written about value transformations. What exists is theoretical, often incomplete, and not very practical or real life. I want this to be the practical guide that makes you want to do this.

What I mean by simple, practical, realistic, and powerful

It is easy to get lost in the terminology of value. How can a senior executive with a budget look at a complex table like the one in figure A and decide the best course of action? That is a symptom

Abbr.	Method	Author and year	Publication
CVM	Customer Value Models	Anderson and Narus 1998	Harvard Business Review
CVA	Customer Value Accounting	Gale T. and Swire J. 2006	The Journal of Professional Pricing
EVA	Economic Value Analysis	Hinterhuber 2004	Industrial Marketing Management
EVC	Economic Value to the Customer	Forbis and Mehta 1981; Forbis and Mehta 2000	Business Horizon; McKinsey Quarterly
EVE	Economic Value Estimation	Nagle and Holden 2002	Book - The strategy and tactics of pricing: a guide to profitable decision making
EVP	Economic Value Pricing	Thompson and Coe 1994	Journal of Business & Industrial Marketing
IVA	Integrated Value Approach	Schnell and Raab 2009	Pricing Advisor
TEV	True Economic Value	Dolan 1999	Harvard Business School Cases
N/A	The Dollarization Process	Fox and Gregory 2004	Book - The dollarization discipline: how smart companies create customer value--and profit from it
TCO	Total Cost of Ownership	Ellram and Siferd 1998	Journal of Business Logistics

Figure A. So many definitions... which is why I pick one and stick with it.

of the lack of conceptualization. In VBP there is not enough academic research in the field. No one has built on the work of others. Everyone has his or her own practice with its own standards. At the professional level there is no standard or common understanding, so people go to conferences and see people with their own sets of acronyms from all the big firms. They are all inventing their own terminology.

Most who think they are doing value-based work are either not doing it or doing a different version of it. Even the ones I refer to as value masters do it to some degree, but they are not applying what comes out in their value-based marketing. They have no value messaging in their brochures and no value data on their websites.

I've made this simpler.

We need to fix this and introduce more standardization. What is value management? What is value as a whole, even though the definition of value itself is totally fuzzy? The definitions I use in this book are better, because I didn't invent them. I derived and distilled them from concepts that global consulting firms such as Monitor and Deloitte have tested and proved in engagements around the world. This book builds on breakthrough work that Tom Nagle and the team at Monitor began a couple of decades ago.

I am not pretending to be the inventor. I just want to have one definition. It may not be the best in an academic sense, but it gets through to people in real life. That is what matters.

I've made this practical and realistic.

The transformation I described is analogous to an umbrella that covers the organization. It is a program. It would be silly for me or anyone else to come in and offer a quick talk and a brief set of sessions and all of sudden you have "value pixie dust" everywhere with all of your processes improved. This is not a fix or a magic potion. It is an essential corporate program.

You may have undertaken or participated in other corporate programs, such as Six Sigma. The difference is that Six Sigma was adopted. A value transformation is incrementally assimilated. It becomes an inseparable part of the organization, and you have to make it your own, from the processes to the storytelling. It is not a switch. You need to understand the concepts, customize them, and bring them into the fabric of your company using your own definitions.

You don't go from a cost mindset to a value mindset overnight. It just doesn't happen after a one-day training. Trainings can plant a couple of seeds, but this is a massive and worthwhile undertaking. A lot of people don't necessarily get that message. Other people are skeptics and will fight any efforts to change the go-to-market approach, especially in times of uncertainty.

Everyone in your organization needs to share the same knowledge base. Otherwise you can't do a transformation. The professional buyers are getting more and more training and making greater investments in the science of what they do. Compared to what sellers are getting trained on, it's night and day. If you have a seller selling to a professional buyer, they are getting beaten up by someone who has been trained to beat and break down a value-based offer. Buyers reinforce the commodity mindset, decide who gets what and when, seek greater access to your cost structure and information, and want to control their interactions with you.

I've helped others harness the power.

Now is the time to get started.

The commoditization in products is well underway, and there is always someone who can do it cheaper on the manufacturing side. If you used to struggle when your value came from a product, imagine the complexity when you have multiple sources of value, all interconnected. You have bundles? You want to introduce new services? What is their differential value?

The answer is not about survival. It is about power. This is what winners do in the 21st century. That is why GE is investing so much in industrial Internet. I see it over and over and over: how do we dollarize services, which we used to give away for free? This forces companies to pay even more attention to customer value, and it helps them move away from traditional models to new models that unlock the power of value in places you may have never thought to look.

You say you have a premium? Why do you deserve it? You need a solid battleground to defend the premium. Get better educated and more professional, and get every extra dollar you can justify. The transformation in this book gets you started, and it will fire you up to complete the journey.

Structure: Three parts

This book is a combination of methodology and instructions for making this kind of transformation. I offer you a knowledge platform to learn the main concepts and do this better. You can make this your own. That's why it is different. You have to make this your own story. I can help you connect the concepts to reality so that the method is robust. I will tell you the best practices. It works.

People struggle with customer value because there are so many theories and they don't know all the implications and intercon-nections. The boundaries are not well-defined, and they keep moving. The old paradigm was "do more training," and that lasts

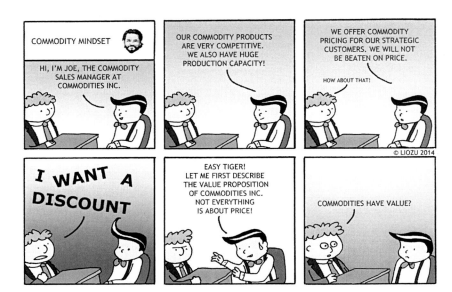

until other problems emerge. This new paradigm approaches this with a transformational philosophy.

Make your own simulation plan and your own definitions. You can bring in a firm and they will do a good job for you, but no one will understand you as well as you, and it takes time. It is a transformation you make, not a strategy you adopt.

I hope I have eased some of your fear or resistance and replaced it with curiosity and a hint of eagerness or excitement.

You can read twenty books and attend eighteen conferences, or you can start with this book. To get this value thinking embedded in a way that people will use it, I give you the best possible methods and foundation, the same ones I coach people to use. I have done the research and vetting and testing for you already.

This works.

There is no secret formula or one-size-fits-all solution. Imposing a methodology in a Six Sigma way will never work. In theory, everyone who uses engineering or supply chain or any repetitive process should be able to use Six Sigma. Value is universal, but there is no universal way to adopt it. That is why it is fascinating. Industries are too different. The concepts and steps are the same, but the challenges are unique to each company and context. Value changes by customer, by segment, by industry, and by source (product, service, experience, combined solution) and against specific competitors. It is also dynamic, as perceptions change daily.

This book is your compass for whatever road you find yourself on. Let's begin the journey.

Value-Based Pricing Is a Methodology

I F YOU THINK THAT value-based pricing (VBP) is simply a mechanical process for setting prices, or a better way to "do the math," let's step back for a moment. VBP is not something your organization does as much as it is something that *defines* your organization: how you go to market, what business model you choose, how you communicate, and so much more.

Before we begin, we have some critical definitions to lock in. These definitions will anchor our discussion throughout this book and serve as touchstones. They will also allow you to understand the methodology by which VBP can become the philosophy guiding your marketing efforts, not just a means you use to set prices.

If you ask a consultant for such guidance, or if you check out any number of books on marketing, you will find too many structures to list here. Besides the 4 Ps (product, position, promotion, price) you will find as many as six Cs. Their heart is in the right place. You can't conduct meaningful marketing work without some framework or structure.

In the course of my many years of work as a coach, training and advising thousands of managers and executives around the world, I have picked up an important insight about all these frameworks. Companies paid them little more than lip service. Their communication materials, the way they presented themselves to the world, didn't reflect the frameworks. Their homework—how they did their math and their research—didn't reflect them either. Eighty-five percent of the companies I have worked with and assessed did a relatively thorough job on only two of the Cs: costs and competition. The rest was secondary, built from guesswork and done in an ad hoc way, to the extent that it was done at all.

You see, these approaches may be elegant and intuitive. They are certainly not wrong in theory. But they share one important and undeniable disadvantage: they are impractical, and the hard facts bear this out. If they were practical, companies would use them regularly and build systems and process around them. Few do. Few ever will.

So here is my suggestion. Let's make our first simplification to allow you to get started on VBP, which means you can rally support and also begin doing some of the hard work. The most elemental chemical structure of pricing—the basic molecule—consists of only three Cs: costs, competition, and customer.

If 85 percent of companies aren't even getting three of the Cs down, let alone six of them, let's fix that first. We can build from there once we have that foundation in place.

The three orientations of price setting: Costs, competition, and customer

Each of these orientations lends its name to a way of setting prices. You have certainly heard of cost-plus or cost-based pricing, and of pricing based on competition. You have probably practiced one or both as your primary way of setting prices. Perhaps you have also done some useful customer research to say that you have covered the customer or value side as well.

These pricing orientations are not mutually exclusive, and each has its advantages and disadvantages. Diversified companies will have each of these orientations to various degrees.

Obviously there are more than three Cs. There are also communication, and capacity, and capabilities. For the basic molecular structure of pricing, though, I turn to a book published in 1990 by Kent Monroe, a professor at the University of Illinois. He looks at customer value, cost, and competition to keep it simple. You have three types of pricing orientations (see figure 1.1). Nonetheless, it is a science, and I will show a practical process for each. Most B2B companies look at cost and competition.

Cost-plus pricing is not evil

It is rare to meet a professional pricing consultant who will not try to talk you out of doing cost-based or cost-plus pricing. I find such comments insulting. Please let me explain why.

I am not saying that cost-based pricing is misguided, simplistic, or evil, which is what a lot of consultants and scholars might tell you. Many companies make a lot of money consistently using this approach to pricing. So I don't want to insult them, belittle them, or call them names. My advice is not "don't do it." Of course you can do cost-based pricing and still be profitable. Some companies

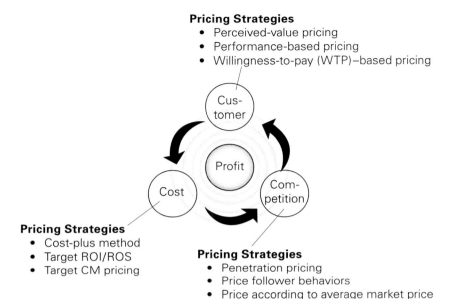

Pricing Strategies
- Perceived-value pricing
- Performance-based pricing
- Willingness-to-pay (WTP)–based pricing

Pricing Strategies
- Cost-plus method
- Target ROI/ROS
- Target CM pricing

Pricing Strategies
- Penetration pricing
- Price follower behaviors
- Price according to average market price

Figure 1.1. The basic molecular structure of value-based pricing: The bonds and interrelationships between cost, customer, and competition.

have developed sophisticated dynamic cost-based models to adjust their pricing dynamically. That's a step in the right direction. The question is: How much money do you leave on the table? If your profit is currently 60, could you do 80? How much improvement is worth the effort?

As economic conditions change, it is important to rebalance between the three Cs. It's not about which one you ignore or discard. Nor is it a question of picking your favorite C. You have to use them all. They all need to work together. They are not silos.

Nor are the Cs mutually exclusive. Think of the situation in a large, diversified B2B conglomerate. The approaches and the emphasis can and will vary by business unit. If the company has thirty divisions, not everyone will use VBP the same way, especially within a couple of years. Each division also faces its own set of external factors. In times of high growth and in times of crisis, you need to move between the three Cs. Know your current position at all times and make adjustments, rather than sticking with one rigid approach.

The C that businesses use the least and which has the most unlocked value is the "customer" C. You don't unlock that value by eliminating cost-plus. You achieve it by adding customer perspectives. The changes you make when you take on the initiatives in this book aren't going to wipe out or invalidate your history. Instead, they mean using what's good and making something better out of it.

What I help people understand, and what this book will reinforce, is that the question for each division is not just "What should be my primary C?" but rather "What should be my primary C *right now*?" The primary C you focus on can and should change, because your market is dynamic! Maybe you need to pay more attention to cost or competition, but at the same time you need to learn to recognize value opportunities—the customer C— and seize them. The "right now" is also just about getting started. If the time is right for you to begin doing more pricing based on customer value, you will quickly realize that in order to accomplish that you need to improve your level of customer intimacy. So the immediacy of "right now" turns into two or three years from now, when you have more customer data, a more intuitive understanding of your customers' decisions, and more funds to continue the transformation.

The intensity and mix and change of each C will be influenced by many different variables. The first challenge for you right now is to manage the Cs better. Only 15 to 20 percent even pay attention to VBP and take a customer perspective. The odds are very high that if you begin learning more about your customers and applying what you learn, you will have a clear competitive advantage over the 85 percent of businesses that don't.

The six steps of value-based pricing: Introducing a formal methodology

Where does this formal methodology ultimately lead? VBP allows you to do simple messaging in front of the customer, but it takes a lot of work to get to those simple messages that you can communicate with pride and defend with confidence.

If you want to charge a premium, you proudly acknowledge that you are more expensive, but then you must justify that premium with your value proposition, which in turn derives directly from your value drivers and your value modeling. Or you can argue that you are cheaper than your competition because of the value you add and how you express it to gain an advantage. You use rational arguments and tangible evidence expressed in dollars and cents, not wishful thinking and pie-in-the-sky selling messages. You rely on your value drivers and your value propositions.

To walk in to the C-level of the entire organization and say *"you have to start doing VBP right now"* is kind of absurd. Don't buy in to the T-shirts with the fancy slogans or read the books that proclaim VBP as something you just do quickly with little ramp-up time. You don't drop what you're doing, turn on a dime, and start focusing intensely on your customers to the exclusion of costs and competition. That is the wrong answer to the wrong question. Here are some of the "right" questions you need to answer first for your customers:

- How much can I shorten their time to market?
- How much downtime can I prevent?
- How much money can I save them?
- How much additional revenue and profit can I generate for them?

Regardless of the question, you need to express the answer, the value, in hard, defensible dollars and cents.

How well can you answer those questions right now? Keep them in mind. Write them down and watch how your ability to answer them improves steadily as you move from chapter to chapter through this book.

Figure 1.2 shows the six steps that will lead you to VBP in your organization. You will immediately see that this is not a light switch, a magic potion, or a silver bullet. It involves a journey of discovery about your market and the value you add to it. These

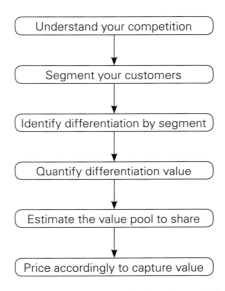

Figure 1.2. The six steps of value-based pricing.

are the six steps I train managers to take in their own firms, after I give them a readiness assessment. The core of the book builds on these six steps.

To understand this process, you must understand the definition of customer value. More precisely, you have to understand the definition of differentiation value. VBP is not about the *highest* price you can achieve, but rather the *right* price for the value delivered versus your competitors. Right now, without the customer perspective, you can be totally underpriced or overpriced. That is the risk that consultants and scholars often cite when they criticize a focus on cost-based or competition-based pricing at the expense of customer-based pricing. But you need to consider all three. The only way to judge whether you are properly priced is to know the value you deliver to your customers and how to share that value. Figure 1.3 is an overview of this concept.

Value can be anywhere nowadays. It often lies far beyond what you immediately perceive. Look for it! As companies innovate and add complexity, it is up to the marketers to find the tangible and

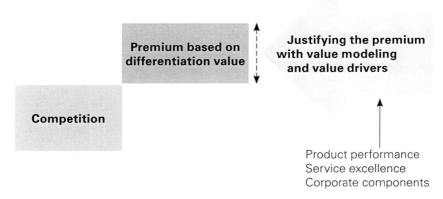

Figure 1.3. The key phrase is differentiation value. How high is yours?

intangible pockets of customer value these companies create. That is the mission of marketing, its way of contributing to the company's success. That is also why getting to VBP is not a copy-and-paste exercise or a silver bullet. While it is possible to learn from what others have accomplished (hence, this book!), each company's value and each company's desire to share it is unique to that company. Each situation is unique. There is no such thing as copy and paste. Nor are there any guarantees of success. I often begin the process of identifying and dollarizing differentiation with a specific customer only to demonstrate that their differentiation level for some products is weak or even negative. For other products or services, that differentiation is much more positive. Until you start this process, everything is theoretical. You do not know your differentiation value until you get into the details of customers' perceived value and until you begin to build these models.

So, you have to do these steps for yourself, on your own, and repeat them, because your market is always changing. I can't do that work for you, nor can I give you any of the answers in advance.

The impact of value-based pricing: Why you should care

The overall goal of VBP is not better pricing per se. The goal is a more sustainable, successful, agile, and focused business. That you price your products and services in line with the value you deliver, and that you reap the financial benefits of doing so, is one important outcome of this process. But it is not the only one.

The figures you will see tossed around by consultants and academics offer you some insights into the potential financial benefits of VBP. Most of them begin by stating something like "a 1 percent improvement in your pricing will lead to an improvement of X percent in your profits." Others will say that their pricing consulting engagements will help you improve your return on sales by between, say, 2 and 4 percent. They may even offer some examples to back up these claims.

The consulting firm Monitor says it can use pricing to help companies achieve an incremental 8 percent, and McKinsey comes up with all sorts of similar numbers. But it is difficult to speak to a number or to build your initiative with one of these numbers in mind. I could promise 2 percent and you could get 32 percent or you could get 9 percent, or you could get nothing in some periods, because of two facts: your market is constantly shifting, and value is relative. There is no escaping those two facts. Think of it this way: if you were to begin a two-year consulting project right now, at this moment, you would be implementing the results in 2018. Could you sit down right now and tell me what your market will look like in 2018?

So let's get a few pricing secrets out in the open.

First, there is no secret formula; nor is there a special target to measure yourself against. The success of VBP and the precise financial gains it generates depend on so many factors that no one can make any promises before the work begins.

Second, you will have to expect short-term pains to get the long-term gains. As I discuss in the back section of this book, that hard work—the fear of it and the unwillingness to endure it—are two major factors in why people either drop a VBP initiative in its early stages or never undertake one at all. It is true that VBP requires investment that may yield little or no return. I am honest and up front about that. Undertaking and performing VBP means taking risks. One risk is the ability to make a direct, one-to-one attribution for any improvements you make.

It's difficult to calculate the ROI of pricing, but that shouldn't discourage you. The attribution question is big. Even if you break down other barriers to launching a VBP initiative, we have to address that skepticism. Yes, it is hard to measure impact. You can attribute the dollars, as consulting firms do, but ultimately they are citing averages. That means there is a distribution around those numbers. If someone claims that a 1 percent improvement in pricing yields an 11 percent improvement in profit, it could mean that one business or division gets 20.9 percent and another gets 1.1 percent. That is not only appropriate, it may also be all that the respective division could have achieved, given the market conditions it faces. Not everyone shares the same improvement potential, no matter how optimistic the team is.

My advice, again, is to avoid getting caught up in all the "should be" numbers reported. You should have a realistic expectation of improvement weighed against a reasonable investment. Success is not always a question of more money.

There is no secret formula, and success depends on many variables and assumptions. So be careful setting expectations. Don't overpromise. You can provide decision makers and teams with ranges you want to target, but the best indicator is your own empirical evidence. At some point, you focus on pilot products and product launches to get your own base for measurement. Then you can slowly ask for incremental investment.

The bottom line is that you may have to invest up front to enjoy deferred gains. You are making structural changes that may take time to pay dividends. You are not implementing a quick fix or turbocharging something. The investments you make also depend on where you are on the maturity curve regarding pricing.

Here are some additional questions to ask yourself regarding that third C, the customer value one. Have you ever done market studies or voice-of-customer studies? Do you have a positioning analysis you can retrieve and show me right now, which means that you have it at your fingertips and actually use it? Do you have satisfaction scores? If you want to know what your clients want, you need a budget. You need to spend some money to get answers to that third C. That is another fact you cannot change.

My pricing capability assessment includes a readiness assessment. When I begin coaching a team through the process of achieving VBP, I give them a roadmap. In my experience, some companies are not ready to proceed. They are not mature enough, meaning they have little or no experience in communicating directly with their customers, compiling that information, understanding it, and acting on it. Of course their salespeople may have considerable experience with customer interaction—it is essential to their job–and I have the utmost respect for these teams. Nothing happens in a company without the support and action of sales.

But here are three problems with all of that knowledge. First, it is individually useful for the salesperson, not *collectively* useful for the organization. Second, there are questions and observations that are essential to determining the differentiation value you offer, and sales teams may not have these factors on their radar screen. Third, purchasing in B2B companies has undergone a transformation over the last two decades that renders it unrecognizable to late 20th-century buyers. They are armed with the training, the data, the tactics, and above all the *desire* to wring out price concessions, neutralize selling arguments, and, in the case of sophisticated, partner-oriented buyers, achieve a fruitful partnership on the most favorable terms possible.

I recommend that these companies who want to do VBP spend time building their own arsenal of data and knowledge about value. In the following year, they can spend where it makes sense and begin their VBP execution with innovations rather than with established products, whose situations are liable to be harder to correct in the short term. VBP really is customized based on where you are, your knowledge and maturity, and the dynamics of your market. An out-of-the-blue approach won't work if you want a faster revolution. It will backfire, because you will just confuse everyone and set yourself back. Ease yourself into the C habit, and accelerate later when you have established a better basis. There is approach, and then there is **approach.** Do you want to change only your product price-setting process, or do you want to launch a value transformation across an entire business? The scope of your project will force you to choose between different approaches, different levels of investments, and different "sacrifices." For example, I coach and support many organizations with their value transformations. We often start these projects and quickly see a need to negotiate better and to begin saying "no" to discount requests. This then becomes a leadership question: Is your leadership willing to lose short-term volume while maintaining or growing margins? What is their appetite for market share loss? As you can imagine, this is not as easy as saying "let us do VBP now."

"Something is better than nothing"

VBP success is a matter of degree. It is assimilated, not adopted; so naturally it involves a progression, not a binary outcome. While I insist that teams make a long-term commitment to pursuing the VBP programs and enduring the occasional setback, I am also realistic. You have to design VBP based on your culture. That is the big difference between adopting a standardized program (such as Six Sigma) and making a customized organizational change in the ways you create, communicate, and capture value.

I'm a Six Sigma green belt, so I know both perspectives well. In the research conducted as part of my PhD work, I learned that VBP requires a slow, progressive assimilation. In contrast to Six Sigma and other transformational programs you can adopt, VBP is not a matter of standardizing inputs and expecting the exact same objective output every time. The concept of value is subjective, dynamic, and complex. It is about perception and interpretation. It is built on trust as well as facts. It is a trade-off between benefits and sacrifices. It has many dimensions: products, services, tangible and intangibles benefits, at industry level and company level. Finally, value is not absolute. It is relative to competitors, which means you couldn't exclude or ignore the competitor C even if you wanted to. Sometimes your competition is a do-it-yourself solution, not another business. Changes in competition mean that customer perception also changes.

It may be hard enough to get support inside your company for such an effort. It is even more important, obviously, that your customers also believe in your value. I would be immensely pleased if your sales teams were in a position to communicate statements like this one with confidence, and defend it with hard evidence: *"In the last two years I delivered $2 million in products and services to you, and you paid a premium, but you still saved money."*

Every word in that statement tells. First and foremost, the demonstration period itself takes time. You can't go in to even the most naïve customer and claim that the next day you will suddenly deliver value. That would be a kamikaze act. Buyers are not stupid, and you will lose credibility.

Customer value is
- A subjective concept
- Dynamic in nature
- Perceived and interpreted
- A trade-off between benefits and sacrifices
- Multidimensional
- Relative to competitors
- Segment-specific
- Future-oriented

Figure 1.4. This is why customer value is so complex, yet so important.

You have to start projecting the dollarization of value over time. The promised savings in the pipeline are all in the future. When you start ramping up and make a promise, how do they know you will deliver on it? Do they trust you? Can you demonstrate past experience?

In lieu of previous experience to fall back on, you will need the discipline to track value, communicate it to customers, and reassure buyers and stakeholders that yes, this is new, but together you will track the value. Most companies don't have that discipline and therefore do not do that tracking well. Yet it is important for value and a tremendously critical aspect of value selling. You have to track value over time so you can start to move customers and stakeholders to a current expectation rather than a future expectation.

Some things to keep in mind

We began these chapters with lots of unusual statements about VBP and what pricing consultants might say or do. My intention is to give you a realistic and practical view of how to do VBP. Here are some key learnings:

1 **Adopt a methodology and stick with it.** Make sure it is one that is commonly adopted and well published.
2 **Build a strong and aligned knowledge foundation.** Align perceptions, language, expectations, and motivations across all functions.
3 **Make sure you provide a realistic view of what is possible "right now" and what is not possible.** Do you have the right level of marketing excellence? Who is driving the need for VBP? Is the market ready now? Would you be the first ones to start such a transformation in your industry?

4 **Do not fall in love with the theory and concepts of VBP.** Focus on its practical and realistic sides. Much written in the area of VBP cannot be implemented or executed. Nor can good ideas be copy-and-pasted. A success story from DuPont or 3M might turn into a nightmare for your company! Beware of irrational benchmarking.

5 **Start slow and accelerate later.** Once you've demonstrated success and impact, you can bring others in your organization on board. VBP cannot be rushed. It needs to be done as fast as your organization can assimilate it. Study your culture carefully.

2

The Unique Complexity of Value-Based Pricing

THERE ARE MANY MYTHS *and misperceptions about value-based pricing (VBP) that make it hard to appreciate and hard to sell internally as an initiative. Perhaps in the interest of simplicity or expediency, people have watered down the definition or applied it to other concepts entirely.*

So before I dive into the unique complexity of VBP and generate some more excitement about the idea, we must be clear on what VBP isn't. It wouldn't surprise me if some of these myths and misconceptions have discouraged you from pursuing VBP. It is time to set the record straight about these seven myths.

Myth #1: VBP means charging the highest price. VBP is not about having and maintaining the highest price. It is about pricing relative to the value you create for customers. If you bring zero value, don't expect to exact a higher price. If you have higher prices, over time a customer may realize that they are paying too much for the value you deliver. If they don't come to that realization themselves, you can be sure your competitors will tell them. The corollary to this is that VBP automatically results in higher prices. This may occur, but I have seen so many cases where companies overpriced their products and services and either lost customers or left themselves vulnerable. So VBP does not mean switching to kamikaze pricing behaviors such as raising prices overnight. As you will see later in the book, VBP involves many steps and potential challenges, ranging from value creation to value capture. In the end, we are seeking small pockets of value capture that might add up to a significant overall impact.

Myth #2: VBP and premium pricing are the same thing.
VBP is also not the same as premium pricing. I recommend that you avoid the word "premium" because it reinforces the perception that your prices are higher by default rather than higher because you consistently deliver superior value relative to your competition. Premium is relative to competition. VBP is based on differential value versus the competitor. These are two different things.

Myth #3: VBP is synonymous with total cost of ownership (TCO). VBP is not the same as TCO. You only need to look at the "C" to understand why. Offering a customer a lower TCO is purely a cost calculation, but you may deliver value in many ways beyond mere cost savings. Your products may help your customers grow their business, and that difference in revenue and profit for them has a value as well. You can also make emotional connections that have a value beyond pure cost savings. TCO may be part of your value proposition, but it is confined to the cost aspect only. TBO (total benefit of ownership) is one step closer to VBP.

Myth #4: VBP is merely a training program. No, no, and again, no. You may have to take my word for it now, but by the time you finish this book, you will realize that training is only a small part of what VBP requires. VBP is a way of doing business, not a way of setting prices. I am stunned when people call me and ask "Can you please come in and train our salesforce?" but I can understand the source of the misconception. You do have to train, and many conference programs will have a workshop or a keynote address with "value-based pricing" somewhere in the title. But VBP is a methodology and involves in-depth discussions around strategy and tactics. It is so much more than a mere "learn and apply" approach to price setting. You will see.

Myth #5: VBP applies only when you have differentiated offerings. I list this one as a myth because of misperceptions about what the term "differentiated offerings" means. Most people equate it with high value, similar to the way they associate VBP with higher prices or a premium. Sometimes it is true that a business delivers high value in terms of experience, brand, or quality. But high value is not a prerequisite.

The truth is that every single business has a differentiated offering and is therefore a potential candidate for VBP. If you don't believe me, think about this: if customers keep buying from you, you must be doing something valuable. Go find it and localize it. Your source of differentiation may even be your price. No matter what it is, you have to find it and quantify it versus competition. Thinking you are good is not good enough. You also have to prove it, and that means you should not aim for huge differentials without clear proof that you can deliver on them consistently and reliably. Don't aim for 10 percent if you haven't even found a solid quarter or half percent. There is value everywhere in your company (see figure 2.1). The multiplication and aggregation of the value contributions are what ultimately increase your value pool and add to your bottom line. So don't focus on getting a big bang and making that huge differentiation your primary objective, or even worse, a must-have.

Myth #6: VBP is only for large companies. No, VBP is not just for large companies. The smallest company I have helped start on a path to successful VBP had three employees. Small companies can be highly differentiated and offer substantial value, in the same way that companies with 10,000 employees manufacture products that have little or no differentiation (meaning the company needs to find a source of value outside of its products). The one clear advantage that size brings is more resources, which means such a company may be able to collect and analyze customer information with more depth and breadth. But the important part is to get started and to follow the process. Doing customer segmentation

Customer value integrates all tangible and intangible dimensions of offerings:
- Product and service quality
- Delivery capabilities
- Adjacent and corporate services
- Ease of doing business
- Relationships
- Vendor characteristics
- Self-enhancement components
- Business models
- Integrated system and solutions
- Software solutions

Figure 2.1. Customer value is everywhere! If you are still in business and you have customers, then you have differentiation. Find it and understand it. This is a fact.

can often free up resources for more customer focus. Priorities, attitude, and value matter more than size and resources. "We're too small" is an excuse, and a poor one at that. Just get it done!

Myth #7: VBP should be the first step in your transformation. No matter how enticing it may seem and how ambitious you are, the answer is no. To think otherwise ensures that you are only building castles in the air, as the saying goes. VBP can only exist on a solid foundation in pricing and especially customer knowledge. You might recall from the previous chapter that in my experience, 85 percent of companies lack adequate customer intelligence. Once people understand the concepts of pricing and have a firm understanding of customers and their value perceptions, then you can move on to VBP. Until that time, you will lose people because they lack the foundational pricing skills and customer knowledge. VBP requires you to be good at what you are doing today. You have to have some level of operational excellence. Lots of firms that are differentiated cannot fully manage complexity and are not excellent at executing strategy. You will see later that you must have a strong foundation in place before you extract your true differentiation and focus on getting more value for it. These requirements are called must-have for a good reason.

My recommendation for a first step is to become better at cost-based pricing and to do a more informed, intelligent job of competition-based pricing, then slowly build a foundation in value. In other words, the first step is to get more from what you already have, and to become smarter and more efficient at it.

If I can help a company get better at competition-based or cost-plus pricing, it immediately creates two benefits: they have more resources (because of higher profit), and they get used to knowledge-driven and data-driven improvement. This is crucial. They get better *and* smarter. So when the time comes to add in that third C, they have a better basis to build on. You can't go from a familiar zero to an unfamiliar 100 instantly. I understand that and try to convey it openly, which is why I am a coach and not a consultant.

I often help B2B and industrial companies that have a strong manufacturing mentality and technology focus. In these companies, the switch from product-centric to customer-centric strategies does not happen overnight. It takes a while to train product managers, bid managers, sales managers, and technology managers to think about customer needs, customer benefits, and customer perceived value. That is also why I feel perfectly comfortable telling managers and executives that they are not ready to start on the path toward VBP. I can say this because I am not selling consulting engagements. I am an evangelist for VBP, but I am not a demagogue.

The pillars of value-based pricing: Why it is more than a pricing strategy

These myths contribute to the idea that VBP is something you can bolt on to your current pricing practices. You negotiate or set prices on a regular basis already, right? Some companies change their prices several times per day. So if the type of pricing you do changes from "cost-based" to "value-based," that sounds like it is merely a matter of perspective. You use a different set of inputs in your algorithms, and voilà! you have better prices.

There is a small kernel of truth in that statement, but it is still misleading for two reasons. First, VBP means using *additional* inputs, rather than different inputs. Most companies use costs and/or competitive price levels to set their prices. That is valuable input that is also essential to VBP. The challenge lies in getting the additional inputs.

To practice VBP, you need much richer and more current information on your competition. If you have data that is several months or even a year old, it is probably obsolete even in markets that do not appear to be very innovative or dynamic to an outsider. My experience also shows that competitive data is fragmented and most likely stored in people's heads. You must have practices in places to track this competitive information and keep it current and useful. You also need to define your segments and know them well. This means needs-based segments, not ones based on superficial factors such as geography or company size (small, medium, large). Only then can you begin to define and extract your true differentiation in your market, by segment. What you deliver in terms of value will differ from segment to segment, which means you can't make blanket assumptions about the benefits you provide customers in each segment. Their problems and their solutions are all different, even if the differences are subtle. So the reality is that you start building general customer propositions and introduce your teams to them. This first step often helps people realize the need to move away from one-size-fits-all processes to needs-based segmentation. Again, that takes a while. You can tell them, but it is far better to show them through a practical exercise.

The next step is to take that definition of value and quantify it as precisely as you can, both in absolute terms and then relative to your competition in that segment. In B2B, customer value is a number, not a verbal expression. Buyers can challenge you on semantics and twist around a sales pitch, but they have a harder time when that sales pitch, that value proposition, is based on and supported by hard numbers. Think along the lines of these statements:

- *"Our ability to make you 10 percent more efficient saved you $2 million last year."*
- *"By reducing downtime by 3 percent, we saved you $1.5 million."*
- *"Our products and services improved your turnaround time, which means you could win more bids and grow your business by 1 percentage point more than you planned last year. That translates into $5 million in incremental revenue."*

Each statement cites a source of value generation (the benefit) and expresses it in hard dollars and cents. These figures give you a basis for defining and understanding the value pool, the *additional* money created by the partnership or the business relationship between you and your customer. The negotiations should continue with a discussion around how to share that value pool, because both parties need to derive some benefit from the relationship. It is unfair for the customer to claim all of the value, leaving you as the supplier with no material benefit. There is a name for the art and science of striking that balance.

That name is "pricing." It is also the end game!

But you will notice that in the previous three paragraphs, plus the statements, the word "pricing" never appears. There is a good reason for that. You need to lay a specific foundation before you

Prerequisites for value-based pricing:
- A dedicated marketing team
- Foundational pricing practices in place
- A strong foundation of performance
- A culture of execution
- A compelling burning platform for change
- Value as a strategic corporate priority
- Available budgets and resources
- Time and patience!

Figure 2.2. Value-based pricing has many prerequisites.

can *start* with setting prices. That foundation is the central element to successful VBP. It depends highly on that third C, customer value. This foundation is the missing piece in most companies. It requires investments of time, money, and in many cases political and social capital. These are the foundational pillars of VBP. One does not become intimate with customers overnight.

The cultural and organizational pillars of value-based pricing: The prerequisites

Establishing and maintaining those foundational practices, in turn, is only one of the prerequisites for VBP. It is only one of eight items on the list shown in figure 2.2. The others are primarily cultural and organizational. Not every organization and team is prepared to undertake what VBP will demand.

The first item is the dedicated marketing team. It surprises me how often I witness that companies perform some marketing tasks, but they are ad hoc and scattered across business units and subject to the skills that each business unit may be fortunate enough to have. But there is no consistency and no standards. Sometimes I become the chief marketing officer (CMO) on demand for these companies in order to raise their level of readiness and until they hire their own marketing professional. I take on that role if asked, but seriously: it is 2016, and with the unprecedented access to volumes of current data on customers and competition, how can you afford to remain competitive without a dedicated team with the skills to analyze it and turn it into useful insights? Think of marketing as the R&D of sales, and you'll see what I mean.

Marketing is not merely a communications team that creates cool collateral, manages the website, and writes clever value propositions. That impression of marketing is outdated. A 21st-century marketing team comprises the people who perform competitive analyses, those who help define benefits, and those who translate those benefits into a small number of relevant value propositions backed by data. They create the selling basis that your sales team cashes in.

You also need some foundational pricing practices in place, as I mentioned above. These also require standards and consistency, which you can achieve by creating a pricing council and sharing information and experiences across divisions. The pricing council doesn't sit in an ivory tower and dictate what teams should do. In its most basic form, it facilitates the exchange of information, develops beneficial practices, and encourages consistency. It raises the bar.

The third prerequisite is the ability to meet your promises in the field and on the manufacturing line. If you don't deliver on your promises, then you will find it difficult to extract value. Companies have a tendency to offer price discounts to cover up shortcomings on the product or service side. This practice is flawed for two reasons: First, it masks and perpetuates the product and services deficits. Second, it diminishes perceived value. Fix your issues first, then build your foundation. Fixing the issues is not only a mechanical or manufacturing challenge. It is also a cultural one. A culture of execution to high standards prevents you from backsliding or accepting lower quality in the future. You have to make sure you deliver on your promises; otherwise, you may not get a second chance, no matter how good you may be objectively. Customers won't trust you.

Now we get to some of the stronger cultural, political, and strategic issues. You have to have a burning platform for change in the entire organization, so that people endorse a VBP plan. They want to support you because they understand the benefits and why the change is necessary. People won't accept your "what" if they are not inclined to embrace the "why."

VBP has to be an explicit corporate priority. If value is just another buzzword you're entertaining, don't do it. It will fail. A company's strategic charter usually offers clues to how committed that organization is to value. When I read these charters, I often see talk about operational excellence, innovation, ethics, and sustainability. But where is the word "value"? Where is the phrase that I rarely if ever see: "differentiation value?" You can't assume that value magically or organically emerges through all of your other actions as a company. You have to identify it explicitly, and you have to measure it.

You need money and time. If you have a shoestring budget or no formal budget commitment at all, don't do it. You will only create disappointment. You also need time and patience. It may take 12 to 24 months for customers to accept your value propositions and your defense of value. To undertake a VBP effort and expect sustainable results in three months is not possible. It will be a house of cards because you lack the foundation and the cement to hold it together. Think in terms of three years, not three months.

Last but not least, I would make one final recommendation to any company or division serious enough to embark on a VBP journey: put your innovation process on steroids. It is better to have a rich innovation pipeline in preparation for what could be tough decisions you need to make on low-priced volume opportunities. If you have increased your innovation rate up front, you can use those products during the deployment to help replace lost sales with more profitable ones.

The challenges of value-based pricing: What stands in the way of success?

Scoping a VBP project can be complicated. One reason is that teams quickly forget that value is subjective. It is relative, segment-specific, and future-oriented. For these reasons, value is always a moving target, rather than a fixed one you can home in on. The challenges of tracking that moving target are many, but they are also rather straightforward (see figure 2.3). The first is skills.

Skills don't appear out of nowhere. This is partially a question of training, but also a question of talent and of reinforcement. One of my goals in my coaching work is to create communities of value champions. They receive a platform on company intranets, create brochures on value, and even do a "value wiki" that keeps the organization focused on the pursuit and measurement of customer value.

You need a progressive segmentation! One-size-fits-all approaches are a waste of time. They mean that you overprice people who don't want to pay for your products and services and that you undercharge people who are deriving considerable value from what you do. You don't know the difference, and that is wasteful and costly. Having a segmentation built around geography and size is not much better, because these distinctions don't reveal much from a value perspective. You need end-user, needs-based segmentation. This is probably the most neglected of the steps I elaborate on in the next six chapters. To get an end-user,

The challenges of value-based pricing:
- Lack of skills and capabilities
- Lack of progressive segmentation approach
- Lack of support from top leaders
- Lack of compensation alignment
- Lack of internal and external communication
- Lack of collective confidence
- Lack of budgets and resources
- Lack of focus on soft and intangible factors

Figure 2.3. Many companies need to catch up before they can undertake value-based pricing.

needs-based segmentation, you need support from top leaders, and you need value champions to get involved. That is the difference between true commitment and mere interest.

Incentive plans can also undermine a VBP program. When salespeople are comped on volume and marketing and management are comped on profit, the consequences are inevitable and destructive. No one gets along. No one pulls in the same direction. Leaders need to have the courage to address this issue early in the process, not when you are 18 months along and ready to implement. You need internal and external communication around value. This is modern, artful, 21st-century communication. It is storytelling, not fact sheets and dull press releases. Do you have the skills internally to do this work?

Some organizations lack confidence. One of the concurrent efforts as you lay the foundation for VBP is to reinforce confidence. This is another place where storytelling comes in, because the hard facts and the data don't sell themselves. You need to develop a team that is resistant to crises and resilient in the face of customer objections and challenges. Without the confidence, you revert to old comfort zones and you are back to where you started. I have seen it happen.

The final organizational challenge is a lack of focus on soft, intangible factors. A B2B company traditionally focuses on products. In today's highly competitive and globally integrated world, the bulk of your value often derives from what your customers do with your product and the faith they have in it, not what your product objectively does. You earn your money through experience, software, and services, wrapped up in branding that creates awareness and provides reassurance to customers. I have worked with companies that used to generate over 90 percent of their revenue from their products. Today they earn almost 90 percent of their revenue from software, support, and other services. The product itself has switched from a revenue generator to a hygiene factor, a precondition for doing business.

Value-based pricing is a go-to-market strategy

I hope by now that you have seen that VBP is much more than a twist on how you do pricing. It is way of doing business. It is the crossroads where strategy and marketing meet (see figure 2.4). In many organizations, these streets run parallel to each other. They appear to head in the same direction, but they never meet. VBP builds that intersection. So, if you are a pricing professional, ask yourself: "Do I have marketing and sales convinced we need to do this?" I often recommend that pricing teams drive the pricing side of the value transformation, but that marketing should lead it. Otherwise, you will run into headwinds, change management issues, and lack of alignment. Do you think it will work?

This change alone makes VBP worth pursuing. But you cannot take the decision lightly and make a partial commitment. The task begins with aligning your internal vocabulary and with getting the right people and the best brains on board from the outset. The pace and the scope are up to you, and they need to be aligned with what your organization can support and handle. Some organizations will inevitably move faster than others, in most cases because they have a better basis to start from.

Value-based pricing is a go-to-market strategy:
- Segmentation
- Competition
- Differentiation
- Customer value modeling
- Value communication
- Value selling

Figure 2.4. Value-based pricing is where marketing and strategy meet.

I recommend that as you read this book you spend time defining the realistic scope of your project. You have to adopt the right methodology, one you can absorb into your business in a way that builds on what you already do, not that demeans or destroys it. You don't have to discard what you have learned. It is your starting point as you move toward this future.

I don't wear rose-colored glasses, and neither should you. I love the practical side of deploying value-based strategies. But I often have to inject a dose of reality in go-to-market teams. My role is to bridge the theoretical and practical sides of VBP with a heavy dose of realism.

I have set the stage, and beginning with the next chapter I reveal the six steps that will lead you to VBP. If you feel your organization is up to the task, you will be excited to read further. This will be hard work, but the payback is there. You have to craft your own journey instead of playing copycat.

Let's continue!

3

Know Your Competition (Step 1)

IN THE NEXT SEVERAL *chapters, we explore the six steps of value-based pricing (VBP) individually. Each one deserves a thorough introduction. The objective of these chapters is not to provide you with an in-depth treatment of each topic but rather to make you aware of the topic, its breadth and depth, and raise issues about it. Competitive intelligence, segmentation, and other such topics warrant full-length books on their own.*

Having said that, you do need to know why each step of the VBP process is essential, what each one involves, and how prepared you are right now to pursue that step.

Myths about knowing your competitors

Your steps toward VBP begin with your competitors. This is the foundation. Many problems arise later on if you lack the right competitive analyses, which means the subsequent five steps toward VBP won't yield the desired results. Customer value is always relative, and what your competitors do is the primary point of comparison for the relative judgments you make. Pick the wrong competitors, forget one, get them wrong, or make the judgment on a flimsy or outdated basis, and you won't have an opportunity to correct yourself later in the process. Success with VBP starts here.

What is your sandbox and your *direct* competition? Your sales teams may think you compete against the low-cost players, while your marketing teams may tell the world that your company is all about premium brands and premium products. This all-too-common situation creates confusion around alignment. It will manifest itself in further confusion when you negotiate with customers. You choose your competitors based on your strategy. If you are highly differentiated, you don't compete against low-cost players. You compete against the other differentiated ones. And vice versa. This is important to establish up front. And that is why you should create value maps and communicate them internally!

Just as VBP itself is susceptible to myths and misconceptions, so it is with your competition. But instead of describing myths this time, I'll list some statements that you may have heard people say within your organization. They signal that you have some homework to do on competitive analysis before you proceed.

"High level is good enough." No, it isn't. Not by a long shot. Time and time again when companies ask me to coach them on value, I find out quickly that they really don't know their competitors. Or they think they know them well until I start asking for documents and benchmarks. Of course they can come up with a list of company names and products. But even if they know who their competitors are, they don't know much about them, and what they do know is fuzzy and fragmented. It is based more on outdated guesswork than on current, codified, evidence-based knowledge. It is also very fragmented, scattered across multiple account documents, bid reports, strategic presentations, and product roadmaps. They lack an integrated approach to competitive knowledge.

The additional information is all around you. Take the public statements of your competitors as just one example. Someone needs to collect the conference presentations your competitors give and mine them for data and insights. You need to get product spec sheets, and you need to circulate them for comments, questions, and input.

When I start talking about competitive intelligence, the first thing I ask is to see the PDFs related to competitors: data sheets, application reports, positioning analysis, satisfaction scores, annual reports, and so forth. The files are skinny. Right there you have a fundamental problem. You must have enough current information to perform apples-to-apples comparisons with competitors. They are who you are measured against. Value is all reference-based and relative. There is no other way around this.

"What is in my head is good enough." This is the silo problem, whether intentional or not. Some salespeople may have useful anecdotal knowledge about the competition, but they stubbornly safeguard that knowledge as their own competitive advantage. They don't enrich it by exchanging knowledge with others, and they work from memory instead of a playbook and a strategy. Sometimes they also lack tools for easily sharing that information.

The last thing they want is to fill out another spreadsheet for marketing!

Information is power. An "I won't tell unless I'm forced" attitude weakens that power, to the detriment of the organization and to the advantage of your competition. It must be the explicit job of someone in marketing or strategy to capture what's in people's heads and make sure it is readily available for value analysis.

Then there is the problem with "good enough." That sets the bar for competitive intelligence far too low. Once again, value is a number, and value is relative to what your competition offers your target customers. If you don't know that inside and out, you can't measure your own value, document it, and convince customers of your story (see figure 3.1).

"We conducted an analysis three years ago." I am always amazed at how many people feel that old information about the

Figure 3.1. Competitive analysis is too important to leave to chance.

competition, or old analyses based on that old information, is still useful right now. The excuse I hear is that "our market doesn't change much" or "our market is not very dynamic." I have yet to encounter a market where these excuses are valid. These are false perceptions that change quickly once teams learn to follow their competitors and their markets more actively and more rigorously.

Any competitive analyses you did three years ago are dangerously obsolete. This is especially true in markets where the competitive landscape has changed through mergers, acquisitions, bankruptcies, or new entrants. You risk measuring yourself against the wrong product generation and the wrong technology. This is how assumptions get entrenched and morph into myths, which are even harder to eradicate when new data comes to light.

You have to refresh your analyses at least every six months. This refresh must be on someone's agenda. Do you stand still? No, you don't. And neither do your competitors.

"Our corporate strategic group has done that." That may be true, but the work they have done is subject to the same caveats I've cited already. How well have they shared the information across the organization? Who is paying attention to it? How current is it? Does it suffer from the "not invented here" syndrome when it reaches the sales department, which spends far more time interacting with real customers? And finally, did they ask the right questions until they got the right kinds of answers?

It is good to do that work centrally. But if it doesn't flow out, it is useless.

"Competitive analysis does not have to be formal." This is what you may hear from the people who will email you a spreadsheet or hand you a printout when you ask for competitive information. Informal analysis is by definition incomplete, and it comes across more as a check-the-box exercise because someone did the bare minimum of research. Competitive intelligence and analysis is too important to do without a formal, structured, ongoing process. High-level information is accurate and interesting, but you really have to get granular. You have to go product by product and feature by feature to understand the value that competitors offer and how it measures up against the value you provide.

Excel creates its own issues, starting with the eternally frustrating question "who has the last version of the spreadsheet?" When you do Economic Value Estimation (EVE), you must have your competitors' latest performance data.

It is time to correct and eliminate these misconceptions. You will have homework to do and will need to put some processes in place. Most teams I work with find this news daunting at first but rewarding once they make some progress. For many people it is the first time they see the tedious process of data collection yield important and useful insights. Laying the groundwork for proper competitive intelligence is an eye-opening experience that whets people's appetite to learn more.

Know your competitors better than they know themselves

It is rather ironic that the first step of VBP is about competition, not about you. This often creates confusion, but there is no substitute for this first step. It is hard in B2B markets to find ways to know your competitors' prices better, but it is a critical step and it is not optional. What needs to change when you hear comments like those throughout your organization? Let's start by understanding the pricing behavior of your primary competitors.

By this, I don't mean what they charge. That comes later. What I mean is a profile that explains why they charge what they do, and how they go to market. Figure 3.2 provides an overview. You will see immediately that the kind of information you need extends far beyond merely knowing who they are, what they sell, and what they charge. Think of this as your competitors' psychological profile, from a pricing perspective.

It is no easy or trivial task to know your competitors—both direct and indirect—better than they know themselves. The question of indirect competition comes up often if you sell software or services and there is no incumbent. In that case, you have to map out the as-is process of how the customers solve or cope with a particular problem today, so that you can define and quantify the value you deliver as precisely and credibly as possible. Managing what is in figure 3.2 is a job unto itself and needs to be written into someone's formal job description. That person or team needs to collect the information and keep it current.

The dimensions in figure 3.2 help you define the landscape, the sandbox, and the "who," so that you can understand and rationalize a competitor's pricing behavior. I use the word "rationalize"

Profiling the pricing behavior of your main competitors:
- Strategic positioning (differentiated/focus/low cost)
- Pricing positioning (leader/follower/cutter)
- Main observed pricing strategy (cost/competition/customer)
- Observed pricing structure (structured/neutral/irrational)
- Observed pricing discipline (low/average/high)
- Behavior in responding to price moves (structured/neutral/irrational)
- Propensity to engage in price war (low/average/high)
- Propensity to hunt for market share (low/average/high)
- Creativity in pricing strategies and tactics (low/average/high)
- Pricing technology savviness (low/medium/high)

Figure 3.2. The pricing behavior of your competitors has many dimensions.

on purpose here. There is a tendency to think that competitors are aggressive, irrational, and unpredictable. In most cases that assumption is false. Any appearances of such irrationality often have a clear strategic or tactical purpose. It is your team's job to know this.

In terms of pricing, you need to know who leads the market, who follows, and in what way (e.g., timing, extent, and focus of the response). You need evidence that helps you answer other questions as well: What price structures do they use? How disciplined are they? How do they negotiate? How do they respond to price wars? How often have they chased aggressively after volume, or low-balled somewhere on bids? Are their responses crude and simplistic, or do they show a level of creativity and sophistication? These are not yes/no questions. You will see a spectrum in each case.

If you look carefully, you will also see patterns and tendencies amidst all this information. Encourage your teams to work on the assumption that what competitors do makes sense. If something appears irrational, that appearance often reflects a gap in your competitive intelligence rather than a lapse in judgment, a capabilities weakness, or a suspicious motive on your competitors' part.

What do your competitors want?

Your competitors will also have goals and motives, both short term and long term. If a competitor or its parent is publicly traded, they have an obligation in most developed countries to document their financial and commercial objectives. These public filings and press statements reveal whether they focus on market share, revenue growth, or profit growth, and whether these goals apply globally or locally. They also indicate what the company sees as the basis of competition in its major markets, how it positions itself,

Some factors influencing your competitor's pricing tactics:
- Source of competitive advantage
- Overall market strategy: scope, posture, goals
- Location of production assets
- Capacity and asset utilization
- Ownership structure (private/public/hybrid)
- Strategic position and orientation
- Formal or informal pricing management
- Strategic assumptions

Figure 3.3. Several factors can influence your competitors' pricing decisions.

and what it sees as its advantages (see figure 3.3). You will often see their estimates, both qualitative and quantitative, about future market trends. Search all of their online reports for keywords. An important clue is where and how often they use the word "value" in their statements. How do they define and measure it?

For companies that are privately held or in less transparent markets, you can still find a surprising amount of information from which you can infer your competitors' goals and motivations. Their websites, their statements in local newspapers, and analyses by third parties are an excellent place to start.

There is some homework and detective work involved. Part of the challenge is to avoid taking everything you read or hear at face value. You need to think critically and look for patterns, because there's a lot of noise in any market. Some competitors are trickier to manage. Your objective at this stage is not to get their price levels; it is to document their behavior and what influences their strategy and tactics. You want to be able to anticipate their moves, and how they would respond to moves you make. You won't find complete and useful data in every case. That only happens in the safety of business school classrooms. You will need to make some assumptions.

If competitors learn that you emphasize differentiated value and practice VBP, you will need to scrutinize your competitors' behavior more closely. They can create rumors and try to disrupt your plans, so beware.

Gamesmanship is part and parcel of price negotiations, especially when the stakes are high. This presents a challenge for your team, to know the difference between gamesmanship and actions that mean what they appear to mean. Are they fundamental changes in behavior or mere tactics? I include some examples of gamesmanship in figure 3.4.

At this point you can already summarize your information in a compact form, which I refer to as a strategic map (see figure 3.5). This format has several advantages. People can read it quickly, familiarize themselves with competitors, challenge the information, and flag points that they feel require further explanation. If you are dumping 40-page reports on people's desks at this stage, you haven't looked hard enough to find the patterns in the information that indicate how your competitors plan to behave.

How do your competitors create value?

VBP is not static; it is dynamic. It needs to be managed mindfully and purposefully, so that people have the right information

Beware of competitive pricing games and tactics:
- Irrational pricing signals and rumors
- Fake price increase announcements
- Provoking of a price war and then withdrawing
- Low bids with competitor's very loyal accounts
- Irrational and confusing pricing actions in the market
- Unusual price response at accounts or in markets
- Aggressive pricing actions to gain share and contracts
- Sudden change in pricing orientation and strategy

Figure 3.4. Competitors don't always play fair. Learn to know the difference.

	Company A	Company B	Company C
Financial perspective			
Return on total capital	4%	3%	5%
Net profit margin	1%	3%	5%
Operating margin	5%	11%	10%
Revenue growth	22%	10%	13%
Customer perspective			
Value proposition	Low cost	Innovation	Premium
Segment/share	Price sensitive (4%)	Value oriented (2%)	Luxury seekers (10%)
Service	Domestic	Regional	Global
Load factor	72%	80%	55%
Primary promotional media	Website/digital	Digital/peers	Clubs/Amex
Technology sophistication	Medium	Medium	High
On-board entertainment	None	Internediate	Advanced
Procurement perspective			
Nature of RFP process	None	Regular	Flexible
Buying style	Irrational	Professional	Collegial
Operational planning	6 months	6–12 months	24 months
Decision making timing	1 month	1–2 months	4 months
Number of strategic suppliers	2	2	1
Risk behavior	Neutral	Taker	Neutral

Figure 3.5. Strategic maps are the kind of behavioral "cheat sheet" you need to aspire to.

at the right time. If you don't form hypotheses about your competitors—who they are, what they want, how they deliver value—then it will be difficult to make sense of any value model you create.

Whether you like to admit it or not, your competitors create a considerable amount of value, just as you do. In most cases, they will be superior to you in some aspects, weaker in others. How do they achieve, maintain, and communicate the source of their advantages?

Once you've documented their goals and motivations and identified their products, you need to examine their value at the next level of detail. You have to estimate your competitors' performance levels and do an apples-to-apples comparison with your products and services, feature by feature. This is a step that I see companies rarely take, or if they do, rarely do well. It requires time and effort and some ingenuity, and it also demands candor as you admit your products' shortcomings and quantify them.

You need to undertake a range of activities to make these apples-to-apples comparisons possible. Cast a wide net for sources of data to get the value assessments that will feed into your EVE model. Figure 3.6 lists several sources of useful information. Look for third-party studies and audits and for reports from independent testing agencies. Sometimes you need to send the competitors'

Estimating your competitors' performance levels:
- Industry associations performance reports and audits
- Independent customer satisfaction studies
- Independent technical assessments and testing campaigns
- Third-party studies: loyalty, net promoter scores, reputation score
- Strategic accounts supplier performance reports
- Online forums, blogs, and social media platforms
- Better Business Bureau ratings
- Online search for litigation against competitors
- Online search for publicly documented failures, recalls, horror stories
- Customer and distributor testimonials/stories

Figure 3.6. You may have a lot of this information. Now is the time to apply it.

products out on your own dime to get the performance differentials or reverse-engineer the products yourself. You need to cite these sources later on.

Beyond these objective measures, you also need to be aware of any qualitative information that could enhance or diminish your competitors' value in your customers' eyes. Are they getting sued for failing to deliver? Have their products been recalled? Do you find horror stories on credible review sites?

The extensive lists of information you have read on the last few pages may seem daunting. A saving grace is that much of the information exists somewhere in your organization already. That is the problem with silos and with companies where people keep this essential information trapped in their heads for their own private use. You have to do the homework, and a lot of the data is already scattered throughout your company. Get a cross-section of people together from throughout your organization—sales, finance, engineering, after-sales service, marketing, and senior management—and go through these questions as a group. In my experience you will be pleased, and in some cases even thrilled and amazed, at the extent of information that pours out from that group.

The next step, once you have your buckets full of information, is to make the value assessments that serve as the basis for measuring your own differentiated value. This is essential to your VBP process. You have to put all the pieces together and draw insights and numbers from the richness of information.

Value assessments: The first reward after all that homework

I haven't asked you to gather all of that information for information's sake. It has a very useful application (see figure 3.7).

	Product 1	Product 2	Product 3	Product 4
Feature 1	✓	✓	✓	
Feature 2	✓			
Feature 3		✓		✓
Feature 4	✓			
Feature 5				
Feature 6	✓			
Feature 7				
Feature 8	✓			
Feature 9				
Feature 10				

	Product 1	Product 2	Product 3	Product 4
Price	$199	$229	$209	$249
Memory size	16 mb	24 mb	36 mb	18 mb
Operating system	IOS	Android	IOS	IOS
Scalability?	Yes	No	No	Yes
Camera resolution	6 MP			
Battery life	10 h			
Battery replacement	No			
Screen size	16			
Storage expansion	No			
Weight	110 g			

	Competitor 1	Competitor 2	Competitor 3
Overall value for money	3	4	8
Quality reliability	2	4	9
Technical support	4	6	6
Ease of installation	6	4	6
Lead time	7	6	8
Ease of doing business	6	4	8
Customizable solutions	2	3	6
Length of warranty	1	6	6
Experience of staff	5	5	7
Accuracy of documents	5	6	6

Figure 3.7. Performance assessments… this is where you start applying all that data.

The fundamental question now is: how do you rate your performance versus that of your competition, feature by feature? These are simple tools you can use to answer that question, often with the same multifunctional group that contributed the data. I strongly recommend that you start internally and gather opinions, even if much of the information is qualitative. It is a mistake, and often an expensive one, to commission external market research before you've exhausted all internal means to answer these questions with confidence. Your organization is savvier and more informed than you think, once you establish a way for it to be *collectively* informed instead of *individually* informed.

One of the most effective ways to document and understand your differentiated value is to make it visual. You can create value maps, such as those shown in figure 3.8. Value maps are not static, so I suggest that you use them dynamically. Move a dot and ask yourself what happens. How will the rest of the market (including you) respond to that move? If you update the maps regularly, you can start animating these snapshots and see the dynamics in your market come to life. You can track trends in perception.

My other strong recommendation in this chapter is this: do not go overboard! Companies often get excited about value maps and

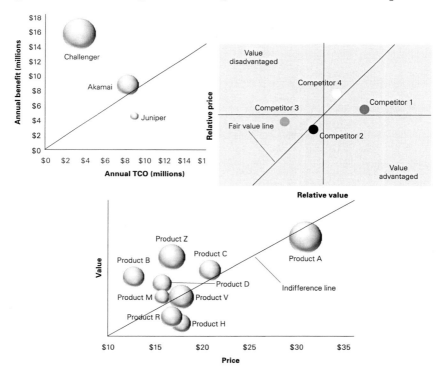

Figure 3.8. Value maps come in all shapes and sizes. Pick the one that works for you and helps your team visualize value in your market and how it changes.

process the daylights out of them. Please don't do this. It is merely a tool. You haven't found religion. Let it inform your decisions, but don't make hard decisions based solely on these maps.

This is why I am not advocating one strict method and giving you "do it this way and only this way" advice. Find a method that allows you to make relative comparisons, then make them visual and dynamic. As long as you meet those requirements, the tool will serve its purpose. That is why I never recommend an overwhelming process. You may have to do lots of these, and update them frequently, especially if you manage thousands of deals with millions of SKUs. The value lies in having a nimble process, not a perfect one.

Tools for conducting pricing competitive analysis

At some point you will need to get pricing intelligence as well. This means data on the competition's price levels. This data is subject to even more uncertainty than the other data you have collected so far. Actual transaction prices in B2B markets are usually confidential and almost impossible to acquire with precision.

Process to gather B2B competitive pricing intelligence (CPI):
1 Assemble and launch a CPI task force (2 weeks)
2 Assign responsibility and accountability (immediate)
3 Conduct an internal audit of what CPI is currently available (4 weeks)
4 Conduct gap analysis, CPI data needs, and tracking mechanism (2 weeks)
5 Launch formal mechanism and process to systematic collect CPI (ongoing)
6 Track progress of CPI collection in task force and pricing council (ongoing)
7 Integrate relevant and credible CPI into pricing decision process
8 Design tools and technology to automate the CPI process

Figure 3.9. Triangulation begins with a team and a process.

The solution is to gather whatever you information you have and then triangulate the answers. Triangulation begins with a team and a process, as you see in figure 3.9. Take a few weeks to gather information you have in-house. What do you have available in-house? Like the other information, it may be in someone's head or filed away somewhere. Sales may know that you usually win or lose deals around certain price points, information that may offer insight into your competitors' targeted and walk-away prices. Other internal and external sources are pretty standard, such as those shown in figure 3.10.

But someone has to do the digging and sifting. You may need to do some external research as well. If so, you don't need to begin with something extensive. You can identify levels from satisfaction studies, do mystery shopping, and conduct qualitative interviews with customers to gain insights into why you won or lost certain deals. This is more like detective work than a formal research study or survey. You have a lot of options for external research, as figure 3.11 shows.

Eventually you combine all the sources and triangulate between the multiple data points. You never take the nuggets themselves as correct. At some point you find a zone of comfort or confidence.

Internal sources	External sources
Historical files	Distributors and agents
Marketing research reports	Independent consultants
Consulting research reports	Customers and end users
Account profiles and visit reports	Online public records
Sales force hard drive and head	Professional databases
Win/loss analytical reports	Ex-employees and retirees

Figure 3.10. Sources of B2B competitive pricing data. Cast a wide net: good data can come from many sources.

Market research for competitive pricing intelligence:
- Customer satisfaction studies
- Positioning studies
- Mystery shopper and customer studies
- Online competitive pricing research
- Qualitative interviews at trade shows and industry events
- Qualitative expert interviews
- Proprietary B2B pricing research with professional research firms
- Online secondary research (public information, databases, etc.)

Figure 3.11. Choose the specific method that will fill your gaps, rather than jumping right in.

But don't pat yourself on the back yet. Prices are also dynamic. Repeating the process should reinforce that comfort level. Figure 3.12 outlines some of the factors I believe are key to success in collecting and processing competitive pricing intelligence.

Having a process means that you are serious about it and that someone is accountable for it. You don't need an overwhelming process, though. Start by being more systematic, and keep gathering data. The process will evolve naturally into a formal competitive pricing process, at which point you can start integrating it with the other two Cs (cost and customer).

Key success factors in collecting competitive pricing intelligence (CPI):
1. Conduct specific competitive pricing research
2. Combine internal and external sources of CPI data
3. Collect multiple pricing data points from various sources
4. Triangulate competitive pricing data for credibility
5. Refine data accuracy and validate to increase confidence
6. Make collection of competitive pricing data systematic
7. Connect all CPI data to customer and cost data
8. Leverage technology to manage CPI data

Figure 3.12. Keep these points in mind, step by step, as your process evolves.

Some things to keep in mind

1 **Most companies focus on competitors in their strategy but do not know their competitors well.** This sounds paradoxical, but it's the reality.
2 **You do not need a team of twelve competitive analysts to get started.** Begin collecting and assembling the data you have available today across your organization. You will be surprised about what exists!
3 **Collecting pricing information on competitors is often considered taboo in the B2B world.** Of course, there are things you cannot do or say about competition. It is essential to stay on the right side of the ethical and legal lines.
4 **Gathering and mining competitors' information is a team sport.** One person working alone cannot do it. The input and the interpretation must be done with all the relevant functions around the table. You have to be able to sort through the noise, the tricks, and the real nuggets.
5 **Excellence in this area comes with practice, collaboration, and discipline.** It will not come overnight, but it will come with effort and resilience. It is step 1 of VBP for a reason. You have to know who your true competitors are and how you are doing against them. There is no other way around the challenge.

My final word...

Don't get discouraged. Get started. If you do very little of this work right now, it may seem daunting. Take it one step at a time, and over one to two years it will evolve. You will be amazed at what you learn and energized by the rhythm you get into. That is why you hear transformations such as VBP described as a journey.

4

Know Your Customer Segments (Step 2)

W HEN I ASK A B2B company about its customer segmentation, the answers almost always fall into one of two categories.

Some teams will say they have a segmentation based on size, geography, applications, product types, or in some cases a combination of some criteria. I will hear "yes, we segment our customers into large, medium, and small companies" or "yes, we break down customers by their locations" or "we have the automotive segment and the health care segment." They will say that their segmentation has several advantages: it's intuitive, easy to do, and data-driven. Other teams will explain that they don't have a customer segmentation, because they invest their resources in solving problems. These are often companies that have a strong engineering focus, and whose very talented R&D teams have discovered ways to help customers accomplish hard tasks more efficiently or more effectively. Many such companies don't even have a formal marketing department, especially in traditional industrial or manufacturing markets.

It is a major wake-up call for companies in both groups when I explain to them that these approaches to customer segmentation are not only inadequate and obsolete but also dangerous, because they cost their companies a lot of money. I am not talking only about the proverbial money on the table, one of the most important incentives for pursuing value-based pricing (VBP). I am talking about real costs you incur right now! Not having a proper segmentation is expensive and inefficient.

The companies in the first group above are using "firmographic" data to group their customers. They adjust their value propositions based on measurable but superficial differences between their customers. That is where the problem begins. A small company can behave the same way as a large one, rendering that size distinction meaningless. A large company based in the US can have the same needs and exhibit the same behaviors as a small company in Asia, which renders the geographic labels meaningless as well.

The companies in the second group are using a one-size-fits-all approach, which guarantees three things.

- **They overcharge a lot of customers.** These customers are vulnerable to attacks from competitors and receptive to their stories about better value. One-size-fits-all companies also lose potential customers who would love to work with them but can't afford them.
- **They undercharge a lot of customers.** These customers see the value in the solutions better than the suppliers do themselves. They aren't loyal because of friendliness or superior performance, even though those aspects do matter. They behave that way because they are ripping the supplier off.

- **They annoy or even anger customers.** This happens because there is a mismatch between what the company communicates or proposes and what the customer needs. It's like Goldilocks. The supplier is either too pushy or too inconsistent and unresponsive, when the customer needs communication that's *just right* in amount and frequency.

This has to stop! It is time for you to take a scientific approach to segmentation and take users' behaviors and needs into account. The key words in the explanations you just read are *behavior* and *needs*. These are the essential components, the essential criteria, for a segmentation that will allow you to do VBP and at the same time make your internal operations more efficient and effective.

Segmentation is the most neglected step in VBP. This is because it is the most complex step and the most difficult to change. Think back to what you read in the introduction. Around 85 percent of companies do not incorporate customer value adequately into their pricing decisions. One of the root causes of this is the lack of a scientific customer segmentation, one that goes far beyond the traditional firmographic labels of the 1980s and 1990s and takes advantage of the rich breadth and depth of customer data available to companies in the 21st century. This is a core issue in B2B and industrial sectors, where knowing your customers is just as essential as knowing your competitors, if you want to succeed at VBP.

The entire field of marketing is moving more and more to science. Given the granular data at your fingertips today, it is getting easier and easier for you to gain a more in-depth understanding of your customer, far beyond the visible firmographic data. You need to know your customers one by one, but it is not practical to have a customized strategy for each one. Your customers would love you for it, but that approach would create even higher costs and inefficiencies and is probably prohibitively expensive to set up, never mind to sustain. So somewhere in between custom strategies for each customer and a one-size-fits-all approach lies the optimal segmentation for your company. The rest of this chapter sets you on the path to finding it.

As I said in the previous chapter, topics such as competitive intelligence and segmentation deserve full-length books of their own. I usually spend a lot of time and sweat equity during the process of customer segmentation. And having deployed VBP in many large industrial organizations, I have many stories and battle scars to show for it. So there is only so much depth and detail I can cover here. In this chapter I provide ways to get you started and get you excited about segmentation. We will look at the unexpected benefits that a strong segmentation will bring you, examine some of the barriers to implementation, and go through some best practices for jump-starting the process quickly in your company.

Traditional segmentation is dead: Long live customer analytics!

The benefits of a strong segmentation

When consultants talk about segmentation, I think they undersell the benefits it brings. They stress only the narrow marketing benefits, such as the ability to target your customers better. That is a big advantage, yes, but it is only one part of the package. I hope the points in figure 4.1 open your eyes to what segmentation can do for you financially and operationally.

Of course I am not talking about just any segmentation. The categories mentioned at the beginning of this chapter, strictly speaking, are also segmentations. We have to distinguish between good and bad. Those segmentations from earlier are weak because

Figure 4.1. The four benefits of segmentation. A strong segmentation is much more than a marketing exercise.

they often achieve the opposite of the benefits shown in figure 4.1. Let's start with leveraging your assets.

When companies try to improve or replace their segmentations, they often make a major and unintentional mistake. They burden the new segmentation with too much change. In some cases, the changes are so far-reaching that segmentation seems like a Trojan horse for smuggling in a plan for organizational change, or as a way to sell an organization on those kinds of changes. Nonsense! Most companies can't shift like that even if they wanted to. It is fairly impossible to ask large industrial firms to get their operations, IT, and accounting reorganized overnight to reflect new needs-based customer segments. Some companies have tried it, and they failed miserably. So it is not a question of revolutionizing your organizational structure to match your segmentation. It is about managing a multidimensional segmentation that aligns your go-to-market approach with your resources to match the customer segments.

I always recommend a hybrid approach to segmentation. You cross your existing internal structure with a customer structure based on usage, behavior, and needs. This leaves your legacy structure intact and uses it to your advantage. It treats your existing systems, data, and people as underutilized assets, not as things that need to be radically changed or swapped out. You can be disruptive without dynamiting your existing structures. I explain more about hybrid segmentations as we proceed through the chapter.

Segmentation can also be a significant and beneficial cost-cutting activity. Let's say an organization has a marketing budget of $10 million. A good segmentation will allow the company to reallocate it to improve the ROI, or to even reduce the budget. You get a bigger return or you save money. You accomplish this by making smart changes to how you approach your customers, in line with what *they* need. One small example: you stop printing physical brochures if most customers don't want them.

A segmentation also boosts customer loyalty, because you improve your information flow. Your customers appreciate their relationship with you more, because they get the right level of attention, which may be *less* than the amount they get today. Finally, a strong segmentation also improves sales effectiveness and performance. You increase the odds that you will close deals at acceptable prices.

Segmentation provides many of these benefits not because you start doing new things, but because you eliminate practices and behaviors that are adding cost, inefficiency, friction, and frustration to your marketing and sales efforts. You can think of segmentation as a damage control program, because it helps you start treating your customers properly and stop annoying them. You stop creating mismatches between the products, services, and prices you offer and your customers' underlying needs. Doing a proper segmentation is not something that gets you from good to better. In many cases it is something that gets you from harmful to neutral. With all of the data and analytical tools available today, there is no longer any excuse for having a bad segmentation or no segmentation at all. Stop treating the damage from a bad segmentation as a cost of doing business that is not worth remedying.

If your go-to-market approach is one size fits all, you are taking a shotgun approach. That may be inexpensive and expedient, but it is also primitive. The symptoms are easy to spot once you have your antennae up: You negotiate too much and too long with everyone. You waste a lot of time and goodwill trying to overcome the inherent mismatch between what you are offering and what that customer actually needs. In addition, you have too many salespeople chasing the wrong deals, in part because they cast their nets very wide. The days of shotgun or mass mailings are history. Think of the traditional industry trade show. A mass mailing means you have invited everyone to the show, even those who don't care. You haven't sent them something valuable. You have sent them trash. Marketing loves communication and loves to make sure everyone hears the message. The savings and efficiencies come when marketing knows who really wants a message or needs it. You match your communications mix to these needs.

It is not necessary to quantify the profit leakages to convince you of the extent of the inefficiencies if you don't have a segmentation. They are apparent once you look, as figure 4.2 shows. Strategic planning suffers as well. You can't set priorities without a segmentation. Your default approach is to treat all customers equally and

Selling without segmentation:
- Splitting time *equally* among all customers
- Favoring the *process* instead of the content because of the high number of accounts to manage
- Visiting price buyers who do not *want* sales interactions
- Not spending *enough time* with high-value targets
- Trying to introduce high-value innovation products to customers who simply will *not pay for them*
- Conducting *marketing activities* with accounts who do not care
- Potentially chasing the wrong *prospects*

Figure 4.2. Look at all the costs you incur when you don't have a segmentation.

to devote equal time to them. Changing this makes some people uncomfortable. If you have a fixed amount of resources, giving more attention to some customers and less to others puts the latter customers at a disadvantage. Yet, as uncomfortable as it may sound, that is a good outcome of a segmentation. Segmentations are by definition exclusionary to some degree.

The flip side of that is giving too little attention to good customers and too much attention to those who are not as strong a fit for what you offer. Chasing the wrong prospect means you are not chasing the right one. Your salespeople will have a sense for this, although they may not have quantified it or expressed it directly. If your success probability for certain kinds of clients is generally low, the answer is not "try harder" or "blame sales." The answer lies in fixing your segmentation, or lack of one. You're investing resources in potential clients with limited upside, which drains away resources from customers who could be more lucrative.

This creates a significant opportunity cost. No industry or sector is immune to this, but it is more pronounced in B2B and especially in semidurable goods. I still see companies in those sectors who define marketing solely as communication. That doesn't work in 2016.

I stress these points because people fear that a segmentation means extra layers of work that never go away or let up. You have more analyses, more decisions, more process steps, et cetera. A good segmentation actually has the opposite effect and should mitigate that fear that the results will only be "add add add." I am not denying that segmentation costs money and that you will need to set money aside for it. But if you do the work right, there are quick, tangible paybacks. It is an exciting shift of mindset.

The challenges to implementing a segmentation

I admit that segmentation can be hard to operationalize. Of all the pillars of VBP, it is probably the one that sounds the greatest in theory but is hardest to implement and sustain. This is one of the reasons why 85 percent of companies incorporate only cost and competition into their pricing decisions and neglect the customer C. There are also some practical reasons why segmentations are hard to implement, as you can see in figure 4.3. I will expand on a few of them.

Internal challenges with B2B segmentation:
- Reliance on *traditional segmentation* criteria: firmographics or products.
- Lack of marketing sophistication, customer *knowledge*, and relevant *data* (qualitative and quantitative).
- Traditional and legacy organizational *structures* that are difficult to change (silos, hierarchy, and roles and responsibilities).
- Focus on 100% accuracy, leading to *analysis paralysis* in technically sophisticated B2B companies.
- Change *resistance* when segmentation is not done collaboratively.
- Lack of *commitment* to execution due to change complexity.

Figure 4.3. Implementing a B2B segmentation requires clearing many hurdles.

Legacy. This is a big one, which affects many more things than just segmentation. When you have trained a team and set up systems such as CRM and other office management software to sort and recognize customers one particular way, it can take considerable one-off effort to make a conversion. One reason segmentation efforts fail is that you try to conduct too much organizational change when you implement it. Use your legacy systems and data to your advantage!

Sales attribution. A second concern, which may affect everything from the pursuit of leads to compensation, is sales attribution. Silos do exist, and they are resistant to segmentation. Customer segmentations that allocate customers across divisions are harder to implement, especially if your sales reps are territorial. A segmentation can significantly redefine territories and responsibilities, which can also alter the status and power of people within an organization. These political concerns, whether we like them or not, are real.

Clusters. A related point is how watertight the segmentation is. It can be difficult to place all customers in clear "clusters" without having some overlap with another cluster. B2B customers can be large and diversified, which may mean that they fit comfortably into more than one segment. Segmentation is even more challenging, confusing, and complex when your organization sells through trade channels, because you need to segment these as well. Segmentation is necessary for end users or end customers, especially when the bulk of your direct-selling relationships are with intermediaries rather than with the people who ultimately use your products. As I explain later, you shouldn't pursue perfection, because you will never achieve it. Get 90 percent of your customers or even 95 percent in the right clusters, make a call on the rest, and then reap the benefits. This is a much better approach than waiting for an extra incremental level of precision that will never come.

Courage. Finally, an organization may lack courage to deploy disruptive structures that can have three or four dimensions. Segmentations have some inherent complexity, which can be a major adjustment for an organization that has kept its structures and processes relatively clean and simple.

Think back to what I was saying in the early sections of the book. If pricing teams are leading the VBP deployment, is it realistic to expect that the pricing function is going to change the overall customer segmentation? Do they have the authority, mandate, and skills to do so? Will they be able to convince sales, marketing, and finance to follow?

First decisions to make before you get started

Before you get started, there are some key considerations to discuss and validate.

1 **Do you want to segment the entire market population, or just your customer base?** This is an essential question to resolve. If you decide to list all market players, you will have to include current customers you sell to (active), current customers you do not sell to (passive), potential prospects, and other accounts that might be future targets. I often begin my segmentation work with current customers and then end up with a long list of market actors. I can double the number of accounts to include in the analysis. It also makes everyone realize that there are accounts we forgot about, that we

never visited, or that we have no clue about. It ends up being a wake-up call for marketing and commercial teams that we do not understand our key population well. Including all these unknown accounts and prospects enriches the analysis and allows us to find trends and future accounts. It also adds a lot of work up front to the segmentation. So you have to decide this first.

2 **Do you focus your segmentation analysis on your core group of active customers, or do you include these customers who are not strategically a fit for your business?** Often, B2B companies will define their sandbox based on strategic fit. They might leave small customers to distribution or refuse to sell in some commoditizing market verticals. Here are we are faced with the same trade-off as in point 1. The more you include in the analysis, the more work you have to do. The issue here is that a nonstrategic vertical today might be very prosperous and attractive five years from now. Or disruption might be happening in a nonstrategic section of your market that might impact your core segments.

3 **Finally, do you exclude from your segmentation work the customers or prospects who would never ever consider your products, services, or innovations?** That is another critical decision to make before you embark on a deep customer-segmentation analysis. For example, if you sell very high-end technology, do basic unsophisticated accounts belong to the core customer target group?

There is no right or wrong; there are decisions to make up front. You have to stay agile in your approach, though. You might realize that your initial approach and scope is not robust or wide enough. You then might have to extend it later or refocus it. My preference is to structure the process by including as many accounts and prospects as possible. Understanding your market population and characterizing your entire account list brings a lot of value if you have the time, the resources, and a salesforce willing to support the process. If you are in a hurry and need focus to support short-term decisions, then concentrate on your core customer segments and your active customers. Remember the garbage-in/garbage-out principle. Are you doing this analysis to make a process owner happy and to check a box? Or are you doing this analysis to seriously rethink your go-to-market approach and to follow it up with concrete actions?

Best practices for stronger segmentations: Let's get started

The field of segmentation lacks research, content, and knowledge. This may explain why it is so neglected. Companies have few benchmarks, best practices, and generally accepted principles to go on as they plan their own approach. I am working hard to change that.

Scientific segmentation does not mean one narrow approach with many obligatory steps. Dictating one technique is not in the spirit of this book, as you have probably sensed by now. Segmentation approaches range from "doing nothing" to integrative segmentation, as shown in figure 4.4. The closer you can get to the level at the bottom of the figure, the better your VBP will ultimately be. And you will get better at doing segmentation when you adopt an agile and iterative approach to the process. Teams must learn to look at customer segments based on needs and behaviors and to link those segments to a go-to-market approach they can execute. It takes time, patience, and collective mindfulness. Sometimes teams are used to receiving processes and methods all packaged centrally or by consultants. They are more comfortable deploying

Segmentation Types	Description	Examples of variables
Geographics	Divides market into geographic units	Country, region, city
Demographics	Divides market based on demographic values	Age, gender, income, education
Firmographics	Divides market based on company-specific variables	Sales, SOW, company size
Behavioral/ product usage	Divides market based on how customers buy and use the product	Website loyalty, prior purchases
Occasion (situational)	Divides market based on the situation that leads to a product need, purchase, or use	Routine occasion, special occasion, part of day
Psychographics/ buying styles	Divides market based on lifestyle or buying styles	Personality (laid-back, type A), buying style (price/poker/value)
Needs-based/ benefits	Divides market based on benefits or qualities sought from the product	Convenience, economy, quality

Figure 4.4. Segmentation is a science! The more science you apply, the better your segmentation.

those. That is not going to happen with segmentation. It requires collective exploration and design, so that there is a strong level of confidence when it is applied in commercial processes.

So let's catch up! Doing and implementing a customer segmentation is "easier" than ever with all the data available today. Your customers have different needs. If you have not done a proper segmentation, here is another undeniable mathematical truth: you will overcharge some customers, undercharge others, and risk upsetting some. Lack of segmentation is a major root cause of customer dissatisfaction!

Segmentation is a science. You will need data. In terms of behavior and needs, there are some fundamental questions that will help you develop your segmentation. Does Customer A want value or price? Do they want a service relationship or a full partnership? What I've seen in practice is that sales has a visit agenda and they will treat customers all the same. Instead, you need to look at how they buy your products, not just how they use them. What are the occasions that lead to a purchase? How much do they buy, and when? Are they professional, or more ad hoc?

The reality, though, is that the data is not going to create itself or show up on its own. Data might be scattered in people's head, across several laptops, and in centrally located databases. If the data is not readily available, you will have to go find it and start the process this way:

1 **List all of your customers (existing, prospect, never visited).** That list will come from your ERP or CRM platform. Or you will have to assemble it from scratch.
2 **Define classification criteria and begin characterizing these customers.** Do this in a spreadsheet using input from multiple sources: firmographics, usage, nature, buying dynamics, volume, and so forth. These are usually discrete variables that are "easier" to find. The salesforce will help you define the key variables to use and populate the spreadsheet.
3 **List customer need criteria and rate the importance of these criteria for your customers.** In general you can do this on an importance scale of 1 to 10. These ratings are internal, and you will need the input of your sellers to bring the voice of customers into the process. The ideal scenario is to conduct customer surveys for this purpose. However, the

internal approach in a multifunctional setting is generally best given lack of time and budgets.

These three steps should help you reach a qualitative segmentation. You will have the basic descriptive data about your customers, their buying behaviors, and their needs across various dimensions. The rest is brainstorming and figuring out how to find homogeneous groups of customers. For sure, getting at their motivations is the hardest task, but you should be able to get answers about each customer if you have the right conversations with your sales teams.

One alternative I suggest is integrative segmentation. Your salespeople know intuitively that there are differences among customers, so use some techniques to start a discussion with them to articulate these differences. See if you can notice some 80/20 rules. You can begin qualitatively and gather some perceptions that are probably rooted in reality once you begin quantifying them.

If you find out that 20 percent of your customers consume 80 percent of your service time, have you incorporated that into how

Typical needs-based B2B segments:
- **A price-focused segment**, which has a transactional outlook to doing business and does not seek any *extras*. They are focused on short-term cost savings. These can also be called *savers*.
- **A quality and value-focused segment**, which wants the best possible product and is willing to pay for it. Customers in this segment often work to high margins, are niche players, or are very differentiated in their strategy.
- **A service-focused segment**, which has high requirements in terms of product quality and range, but also in terms of supply chain, technical support, or marketing support.
- **A partnership-focused segment**, usually consisting of key accounts, which seeks professionalism and reliability and regards the supplier as a long-term strategic partner.

Figure 4.5. To get started, don't make it any more complicated than this.

you set priorities, how you treat these customers, and how you price your products and services? You can look at the extremes, too. Which customers are clearly the price buyers? You have them. Every company does, and they will make up a good chunk of your customer base. Who are your value buyers, the ones who recognize the value you provide and are willing to pay for it? A good place to start is to assume that 15 to 20 percent of your customers are value buyers. Figure 4.5 gives more clues about what kinds of segments you may have within your market.

A third common segment is speed and convenience. In some cases the company has a separate division by segment (such as Allstate; see figure 4.6). They avoid confusing the two divisions.

You're in good hands.

Allstate offers more experience and broader services

esurance website offers convenient and specialized services

Payroll · HR · Retirement · Insurance

Cloud-based payroll, HR, and benefit solutions

Payroll services that are easy, online, flexible, and secure

Innovation, reliability, and quality

Speed, low cost, reliability, and convenience

Figure 4.6. The power of using second brands to address different segments.

Sometimes your brand can't cover more than one or two segments. Trying to stretch a brand across too many segments will muddy your message. You have to make these brands and segments as watertight as possible. If you don't, you risk giving some customers cheap products with state-of-the-art service for too low a price.

If you follow this approach, you can get surprisingly good results that people accept as a starting point for segmentation. You may still do additional work and thus invest in something more elaborate, but this positive, constructive first step has helped salespeople and the rest of the organization get comfortable with the idea of segmentation and its ramifications. The three ingredients needed to make this work are your best people, common sense, and focus. You will have insightful and productive discussions. Even if you use only three segments (price, value, something else), you can get a rough segmentation quickly.

I'd like to close the chapter with a Q&A format to address some of the most frequent issues that teams raise as we start down the path to a segmentation that enables you to do VBP and that yields many additional benefits.

Q: What do you mean by "hybrid"?

A: Sometimes a hybrid approach is the only way to get the organization to adopt a new segmentation and benefit from the guidance it provides. Your company has an established structure and you can't change that, at least not quickly and perhaps not at all (see figure 4.7). Are you organized—mentally, commercially, and financially—by plant? By region? By division? The answers to these questions often determine profit-and-loss responsibility and resource allocation. It is unrealistic to change this setup.

Figure 4.7. The hybrid segmentation process.

Q: How detailed should we get?

A: Doing a proper segmentation requires time, data, and knowledge; but as with every other approach in this book, I ask that you please not fall in love with the numbers. Do not aim for perfection. Falling in love with data is the dark side. This may sound counterintuitive, but the data isn't everything.

Winston Churchill once wrote, "The maxim 'Nothing avails but perfection' may be spelt shorter: 'Paralysis.'" You should also avoid the perfection obsession and a burning need to validate everything statistically with a high R^2. You never get that. It is difficult to get perfect models. The goal is not perfection but rather to sharpen your lens. That means accepting qualitative information. Many engineers can't let go of the need to validate too aggressively.

They use data rigor as a defense or as a means to slow down or kill good progress. You need to get them on board.

You can counter that resistance with some elements of design thinking. Get frequent feedback and treat the implementation of the segmentation as an experiment, from which the organization will learn progressively. You test, you observe, and you form better assumptions as you go.

Q: How do we segment if we only have a small number of customers?

A: Some B2B businesses and even B2B2C businesses have only a small number of accounts. Clients will sometimes ask, for example, how you do a segmentation if the company only has five accounts. My answer is that the segmentation is already done. Each account is a segment unto itself. Your segmentation effort shifts in this case to what happens *inside* each of those companies. Who is involved in the purchase decisions, and what is each one's level of influence? When you add it all up, you may have to manage 100 people in a customer's organization. You can then tailor your personnel to match their personnel. You can't change the people on the customer side. The burden of matching up falls to you. The more informed you are, the better. Identify these key people and develop empathy with them.

Q: How should we name our segments?

A: Another question that may sound somewhat trivial is how to name each segment. This is not trivial at all. The names themselves can help make each segment more intuitive to understand. You should also always use names that are positive or even complimentary. Assume that the names will leak and that clients will

hear what you call them and others. There is a perceived difference in connotation between calling someone a "saver" and calling them "price sensitive." I would avoid using "price" in the name
of any segment.

Q: How many segments should we have?

A: The rule of thumb for me is no more than five, with three to
five segments the ideal range. You need to craft strategies for each
segment, so be careful here. It may harder to categorize 10,000
accounts into three to five groups. But most large companies I see
have between 50 and 500 accounts that make up 80 percent of
their business. Focusing your segmentation on those customers
will make the exercise more manageable and practical, and it will
still provide improved guidance you can act on.

Once you have your segmentation based on your internal information, you could do external research if you like. This means
cluster analysis. In my view this only makes sense if you have
hundreds of clients. If you have fewer than 100, then you should
go one by one based on your available internal data.

Getting to *segmentuition*

Segmentuition is not a fancy term meaning to make college
more affordable. The best kinds of segmentations—even complex
ones—are intuitive. That applies to both sides of the equation.
Internally you can intuitively understand why a customer belongs
to one segment and not another. When customers see your segmentation, it should reflect behaviors, needs, market realities so
well that they naturally self-select the one that fits them best. The
problem, though, is that intuitive is not a sufficient criteria on its
own. There are few customer breakdowns more intuitive than

firmographic ones such as small-medium-large or geography. Yet these are among the weakest and least effective forms of customer segmentation.

Figure 4.8 summarizes many of the external challenges you will face when you start crafting a better segmentation. What you have read addresses many of these challenges, but none is insurmountable or a reason to slow or stop your efforts.

There is no reason why companies should not have strong segmentations. They are indispensable pillars of success, for so many reasons. Take the approach in this chapter to heart, and you can move your organization much closer to the segmentation you need and deserve.

Some things to keep in mind

1 **How well do you know your strategic sandbox?** Some of the segmentation work is already done when a company decides to exclude or include pockets of customers. For example, if your company does not consider the automotive market to be a strategic vertical, then you are excluding this vertical from your segmentation work. Or do you? What happens if you do not study the customers and disruption happens in this market that might bleed into your core segments? Defining

External challenges with B2B segmentation:
- Some B2B markets are highly *concentrated*. The customer population to segment might be very small.
- The B2B *buying center* is multifunctional, and influence is distributed.
- B2B offerings are more *complex* and often *customized*.
- In B2B, *commercial cycles* can be very long, making relationships essential.
- B2B buyers are highly *educated* and very professional, thus making the buyer–seller relationship more *rational*.

Figure 4.8. Challenges, yes, but none is insurmountable.

your sandbox and who you include in your segmentation analysis are key decisions to make up front.

2 **Do you want to do *current* customer segmentation or *all* customer segmentation?** I always recommend including all customers, prospects, lost customers, and accounts that are emerging in the ecosystem. Be holistic up front, and keep revising your scope. You will be surprised to learn that there are accounts you might not have known about.

3 **If you have many important stakeholders in your ecosystem, you will have to undertake the segmentation processes multiple times.** For example, you will segment your dealers, your end users, potential OEM accounts, consultants, and so forth. That adds complexity, of course, but it's necessary.

4 **Depending on the size of your customer population, you will have to use qualitative and/or quantitative methods.** If you have 50 customers to segment, you most likely will stick to a qualitative segmentation, potentially validated through your transactional data. If you have 5,000 customers, you will begin with a qualitative inquiry to define some axes of segmentation, and then you will validate them through transactional and quantitative survey data. I recommended using multiple segmentation methods to cross-validate.

5 **If you wait until you get 100 percent complete, high-quality data, you will never get started.** You will experience overlap, exceptions, outliers, partially valid models, missing data, and the like. Because it is a slow and iterative process, you have to get started and refine as you go. So you have to begin with the easy or clear segments and put this at the top of your priority list.

My final comment may be the most powerful one: make sure you do the segmentation with the salesforce deeply involved in the process and with access to all their information. A theoretical segmentation without input from sales will be shelved and may never get used at all. What a waste!

5

Extract Your True Differentiation (Step 3)

VALUE DOES NOT EXIST *in a vacuum. Your value—the value that will underpin your value-based pricing (VBP)—is always specific to a well-defined customer segment.*

Value is also relative to what your competitors offer to customers in the segment. By now your thinking should have moved away from generalizations (large markets, one-size-fits-all thinking) to focus on these narrower definitions, because these are the keys to your success with VBP.

To make this operational, I start leading you through a progression in this chapter. To measure your differentiated value, we begin by defining the features that constitute your product and service offer. To make this as simple as possible: each feature should provide customers a benefit. For each benefit, there is a mechanism, formula, or metric to express that benefit. In the final step, we convert that metric to dollars. We "dollarize" the benefits you provide, and examine the difference—dollar for dollar—between what you provide and what your competitors provide.

The next chapter focuses intensively on the quantification of value, so in this chapter we will focus on features and benefits, with only some basic quantification to illustrate some points.

Let's get started!

Differentiation: It begins with competitive advantage

You need to be able to speak fluently in the dollars-and-cents language of value, and you need to be able to speak that language in this customer's dialect. But how to you get to that point? How do you acquire that fluency?

Consider the following questions about what you deliver to your customers, day-in and day-out. What makes you special? What makes you unique as a whole? What makes your products unique? Can you be easily imitated? And how well are the answers to these questions expressed explicitly in your value proposition? The answers describe your competitive advantage, and these in turn provide the raw material for your value propositions. Competitive advantage takes three forms: measurable product and service differentiation, market position, and cost/price.

The sum of these is your overall competitive advantage, as figure 5.1 shows. You will never be strong in all three, although combinations are possible.

That is the way it *should* work. Unfortunately, many of the value propositions I see often contain a lot of blah-blah. They often begin with facts that are not compelling or that are even boring, such as "we have 80,000 employees." Who really cares? Although they may be cleverly written and creative, such statements have no clear connection to the source and the extent of your true differentiated value. They don't make transparent to your current and potential customers how much you can save them or how much they can improve their businesses if they work with you and purchase your products and services. That is the level of specificity we need to get to. You can still be creative, but creativity without specifics muddies the picture and makes it harder for customers to decide whether it is really worthwhile to work with you. You need a value proposition supported by a differentiation statement.

Competitive advantage and value propositions are also dynamic. The answers to the questions I asked above will change and evolve, sometimes to your greater advantage and sometimes to your detriment, as any number of factors change. Your customers' needs change, and your relative value fluctuates as you and your competitors launch new products, change marketing

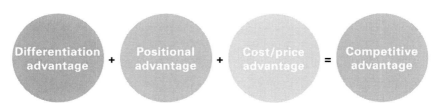

Figure 5.1. Three sources of competitive advantage.

strategies, acquire or shed divisions, shutter factories or announce new ones, or modify overall strategic focus.

As I said earlier, if your business has customers right now, especially regular repeat customers, then by definition you are adding value. You are addressing a pain point, unlocking a way for them to add to their gains, or making an emotional connection with them. And you are doing those three things better than your competitors do it right now. Until you have a precise understanding of that value, and until you can dollarize it, I cannot see how you could build a business model. Ambition and visions are great, but the path to sustained success starts with knowing your value. Then you build a business plan, and then you create a strategic plan.

The idea of differentiation is not new. It has been around in the constructs of economics. I take it one step further by helping you define and express that value in a very rational way, the only way that matters in a B2B environment: Money! *"I save you $1 million in direct costs. I can help you grow your revenues by $5 million. I increase your confidence and peace of mind so that you can spend your valuable time and resources on other tasks."*

Related to my comment above: I am tired of hearing the word *commodity*. Except for standardized items that are traded on international exchanges, such as a barrel of oil or a bushel of wheat, there is no such thing as a commodity. The frequency with which I hear that word usually correlates well with how beat up an organization is. They have given up on value, and they fight aggressively in bare-knuckled price wars instead of making the effort to find and extract their true differentiation. Please let me repeat: If you are still in business today, you are doing something right. You are adding value, and it goes beyond the product. It is therefore your responsibility to find your true differentiation, extract it, quantify it, and communicate it. No one else is going to do that for you. Your competitors are certainly not going to do so. And your buyers are not going to volunteer it!

The VRIO Model: The acid test of differentiation

Instead of burdening you with a complex process you would never use anyway, I recommend a set of four questions as the means to begin defining and quantifying your value. This is an excellent discussion starter that also yields insightful answers to help you recognize and appreciate your own value. Pick what you think is an important feature of one of your best-selling products. Can this feature pass the following four-question test?

- **Is it *Valuable* to the customer?** Customers should be able to tell why they want it, what pain point it addresses, or what gains it enables. The feature is clearly something that makes customers better off, and you have clear, ready answers to describe why.
- **Is it *Rare*?** The fewer options the customer has, the rarer your feature is. You have something customers want, and few others (if any) offer the same feature.
- **Can it be *Imitated*?** In other words, if you gave a competitor a few months, could they perform that same function just as easily as you do, and thus offset or neutralize your advantage? Ideally you would have a sustainable advantage, which means it would take considerable resources—if not a strategic decision—for one or more competitors to challenge you on it. Here we touch on switching costs, which may be technical, marketing, or relationship-based.
- **Are you *Organized* to exploit this differentiation?** Sometimes companies have too much of a good thing. They have the *potential* to offer superior value, but they can't exploit

it, either because they lack the processes to market and support the feature, or they lack the talent or the means to exploit its full potential. Sometimes a company is just plain bad at executing. They have breakdowns in execution excellence and spend their time fixing their issues.

If you can honestly answer "yes" to all of these questions, you are truly differentiated. But most companies will answer at least one question with "no." Figure 5.2 provides an overview. In some

A differentiation value strategy must meet the **VRIO** criteria:
- Is it **V**aluable to customer in dollars and cents?
- Is it **R**are to find or access?
- Is it costly to **I**mitate?
- Is the firm **O**rganized to exploit it?

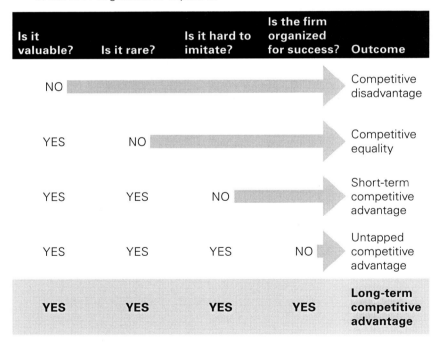

Is it valuable?	Is it rare?	Is it hard to imitate?	Is the firm organized for success?	Outcome
NO				Competitive disadvantage
YES	NO			Competitive equality
YES	YES	NO		Short-term competitive advantage
YES	YES	YES	NO	Untapped competitive advantage
YES	**YES**	**YES**	**YES**	**Long-term competitive advantage**

Figure 5.2. Typical results of a VRIO exercise.

crowded industries, it might be tough to be rare. That is just the nature of the sector. But do not give up. It is what it is, and you will have to fight even more to justify your differentiation and stay above the commodity noise.

Even when you answer "yes" you need to qualify the answer, so I suggest using a scale for your answers. In my experience, people most often overlook the "O" in VRIO. They fail to ask themselves *"can we do this?"* and do not know if or how well their competitors can do it. Are you stretching yourself too thin? Are your competitors stretching themselves too thin? You can't let the data dictate your decisions about whether to go to market with a certain product or feature. Sometimes the most lucrative option is not the best one, if your organization is not up to the task and can't live up to the promise. You have to be realistic and scale things back in those cases, to something you can manage.

The more you go through the VRIO questions, the better you will get at this process. The crucial step right now is to get started.

As you build on the answers to the VRIO questions, you need to keep in mind that differentiation does not always work in your favor. Put down the rose-colored glasses and be honest about how well your features perform against competitors. There is such a thing as negative differentiation, and purely by definition, every company is likely to have some, as figure 5.3 shows.

There is no such thing as "better" without "worse," and there is no "best" without a "worst." It is impossible for any company, even yours, to be better or best at everything. That is tantamount

Positive differentiation: advantage that is generated by your unique differentiators (efficiency, durability, incremental margin gains, etc.)

Negative differentiation: disadvantage that is unique to your differentiated offering (training, testing, ramp-up costs, technical support, etc.)

Figure 5.3. Differentiation can be positive and negative. No one is perfect!

to saying you are perfect, and I don't know of a single B2B market where that is a credible argument. You have to account for the things you are less good at. Focus on finding the positive, but recognize the negative.

What do you do with the answers to your VRIO exercises? You start zeroing in on a more precise definition of your differentiation. Again, to keep things simple and useful, think of differentiation in three ways: "nice to have," "must have," and "true." It is the *true* differentiation that ultimately wins you the business. Figure 5.4 gives you an overview of this hierarchy.

To give you an idea of nice-to-have aspects, I suggest looking no further than the typical brochure or website of a B2B company. Whether large or small, and no matter what continent they are based on, you will see statements about how they have hundreds of plants, thousands of employees, 200 years in business, and so forth. Heritage and brand name are important, but they are the

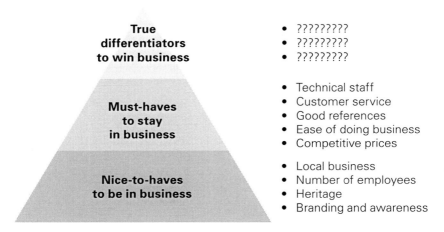

Figure 5.4. Levels of differentiation: The hierarchy of competitive advantages.

usual suspects for nice-to-have. At best they imply that you may be a company that delivers value, but the professional 21st-century buyer on the other side of the table is too smart for that line of reasoning. With technology, professional buyers already know everything about you. There is no need to repeat that you are global, have 80,000 employees, twenty plants, fifteen brands, and so forth. They already know that. In 2015, Forrester reported that about 65 percent of the B2B sales process has disappeared because of technology. There is no need to send the glossy brochure anymore. And I do not think that the beautiful ceramic branded coffee mug is going to make a difference either.

The must-have aspects are the prerequisites to staying in business. You have to have the right technology, good quality, good references, and be someone people like to do business with. People don't buy crap from bad people. Competitive prices are also a must-have, but don't fall into the perception trap that so many suppliers fall prey to and that so many purchasing departments encourage. A competitive price is not synonymous with a *low* price. It is the right price for the right value you deliver. Finding that is the immediate outcome of a VBP process. Your must-haves are prerequisites to staying in business, but they can still help you win if you are significantly better at execution than your competitors are. In some sectors and for some segments, even a must-have can become a true differentiator. The key message here is that you have to have excellence in the must-haves as you build differentiation on top of them. The pyramid will be weak if the foundation is not solid.

At the top you have your true differentiation, the set of features for which you answered "yes" to all four of the VRIO questions. What are these things? Your list will grow as you ask and answer these questions by product, family, and business line. Don't take this process for granted. While the questions themselves are simple, you will be surprised at how many people struggle to answer them. Sometimes your true differentiation—the basis for the customer value you need to dollarize—isn't obvious and right there on the surface. Sometimes it is hidden, and you need to expose it and articulate it in order to unlock it. VRIO is a good acid test that helps you see where your value is and where it isn't.

I have one final piece of advice as you work with your teams to answer the VRIO questions. Avoid spending a lot of time on "if" or "if only…" statements. While these may be a good source of ideas for your research and development team, value is about the here and now. Focus on what you are doing today. What case for value would enable you to close a sale today in a final round of negotiations? Speculating about *tomorrow's* value is a fun exercise, but you need to be disciplined about understanding and extracting *today's* value. This can lead to a lot of soul-searching and many philosophical discussions. It can be sobering to own up to where you fall short, and it can be uncomfortable sometimes to step back from claims you have made in the past and feel you could live up to "if only…" But you need to take this important step in order to do the Economic Value Estimation (EVE) analyses later. Choose someone to play devil's advocate, and work hard to challenge yourselves.

Hidden differentiation: Digging deeper into why you delight customers

A significant amount of your differentiation involves obvious features. Your engine is 20 percent more efficient, your machines have 10 percent higher throughput rates, and your products last 20 percent longer. These are core product features that you can document and compare readily. It is harder to make these necessary apples-to-apples comparisons with services or intangible benefits. Figure 5.5 shows some of the many ways you can find hidden value.

If you want to argue that a service platform such as your customer help desk is 20 percent better than the closest competition, how do you define and defend that number? How do you quantify experience, expertise, friendliness, responsiveness, empathy, trust, and peace of mind? These and the other possibilities in figure 5.5 can be enormous difference makers, especially when you have competitive advantages in several of them. In B2B markets, you have a lot of interaction with customers at many levels. Maybe someone is doing something so unique that it fosters customer loyalty, the kind you earn rather than buy. Maybe your drivers or your training reps are doing customers "favors" that seem trivial and small from the inside but that are very valuable in the customers' minds. The question is the customer perception in this

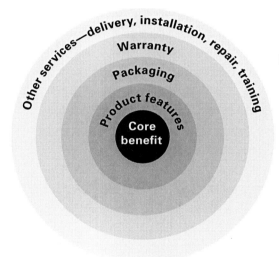

HIdden assets could be in
- Technology features
- Service platforms
- Corporate services
- Unique capabilities and skills
- Business models
- Intellectual property
- Exclusive relationships
- Unique access
- Favors, gestures, freebees

Figure 5.5. Where is your differentiation hidden? You may have a lot of value hidden in your business!

case. You will have to dig deep to find hidden differentiators and for assets you are not fully leveraging. What could those be in your case?

From advantage to customer benefit

You might be better than your competition. The challenge now is to describe that feature in terms of a customer benefit using words the customer understands and the unit of measure that is best for them. This is an essential step of the VBP process. You need this for your value modeling process, because benefits are what you express in dollars. You cannot express feature-driven competitive advantages in dollars. You express the value of customer *benefits* in dollars. You may sell engines, but the customer thinks in terms of vessels with multiple engines. So it does require switching sides and putting yourself in your customers' shoes!

The most straightforward way to do this is to use the 5-Why technique. It literally means that you ask "why?" five times in a row. Every answer is met with the question "why?" or "why does that matter?" until you have arrived at the essence of why your feature benefits customers. Read through the following sequence for a rough example of what I mean. The customer is a small B2B manufacturer with three small warehouses. The numbers and products are for illustrative purposes only:

Your team: "Our lift equipment is 25% more reliable than our competitors"
You (1): "Why?"
Your team: "They stay in operation on average 1,000 hours before needing maintenance, compared to 800 hours for our best competitor."
You (2): "Why does that matter?"

Your team: "It means they have less downtime, and their main-tenance costs are lower."

You (3): "Why does that matter?"

Your team: "If they have three machines per warehouse, they would have 18 extra full days of downtime per year, which would drive up maintenance costs (staff and parts) and also cause dis-ruptions in their ability to ship product."

You (4): "Why does that matter?"

Your team: "We estimate at the low end that each day of down-time costs them $50,000 in lost revenues."

You (5): "Why does that matter?"

Your team: "For the size of the bid they currently have, working with our products instead of our best competitor would enable them to earn $900,000 in additional revenues annually simply because of the longer uptime of our machines."

This example is simplistic on purpose, but you get the point. Imag-ine the difference when your salespeople can walk into the nego-tiation with that business owner and say that working with your company's warehouse machines means an additional $1,000,000 per year in revenue. That is hard, defensible material value that the owner can relate to in his own business context. Compare that with the claim that your machines are 20 percent more efficient, which sounds dramatic but doesn't answer the proverbial "so what?" question.

Reliability is just one of many advantage your machines may have. They may also have some disadvantages. While they may be faster and also process more loads per hour than the com-petition, they may require drivers with more skill who demand higher wages and require additional training. These are offsets to the value you offer otherwise. The only way to understand the total value you offer relative to your competitors is to go feature by feature and be honest in your assessments. This exercise is especially important in engineering-driven organizations, where the culture is more about features than the *benefits* those features provide.

Perception matters: Achieving internal and external alignment

You've done your math and gone into the discussion with the warehouse owners I mentioned above, but they aren't buying what you're selling. Management guru Peter Drucker would not be surprised: he writes in *Managing for Results* that "the customer rarely buys what the business thinks it sells him."

Sure, you are proud of your advantage in reliability, but the owners claim that your main competitor is working on a more reliable machine, and that it said that when it hits the market in one to two years it will offset some of your advantages over the lifetime of the machine. Furthermore, that competitor also stressed its ease of use, which is superior to yours. The owners said they would prefer machines with much better ease of use than yours, because driver turnover is high anyway and they don't see the point in investing in training and higher wages. In the end, from a pricing standpoint it's a wash, and they refuse to acknowledge that you deserve a premium because of your greater reliability. There can be big gaps in internal and external perceptions, as figure 5.6 reminds us.

This situation is not uncommon. Your engineering team focused on higher reliability, you estimated the value of that and made it a key point of differentiation, but your customers didn't see it as being as valuable or extensive as you did and now claim they want something else. What is your counterpoint to their argument? Are they trying to catch you off guard? The point here

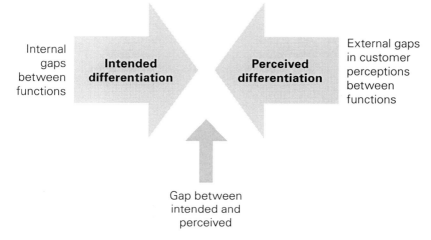

Internal gaps between functions

Intended differentiation

Perceived differentiation

External gaps in customer perceptions between functions

Gap between intended and perceived

Figure 5.6. The case for alignment of differentiation. Mind the gaps between internal and external perceptions.

is that you cannot establish your differentiation to its fullest extent unless you control the differentiation message. It is a communication war. You need to repeat your core messages millions of times, especially when the default message is *You are the same as the others, all things considered* or *You aren't as good as you think you are.* That is what your competitors and the customer buying groups conspire to make you think.

You have to line up case studies, have other customers tell their stories, and use the knowledge about your competitors. What if they missed their launch dates on their last three product launches and even scratched one of the planned products? Having that information could allow you to build some doubt in the customer's mind and increase their perceived risk of going with a competitors rather than you. Doing the math is not sufficient. You have to win the communication battle! Be vigilant and observant enough to know what customers perceive today! Do they know what else you can do or how well you can do it? Is there a third or

The role of your competition's sales force in the market:
- *Pretend* they offer the best value for money.
- Tell buyers they are the *same* or better than you.
- Make the differentiation position *fuzzy* or blurry.
- Tell their *own stories* about you.
- Disrupt value maps by offering *promotions and rebates*.
- Make short-term *promises* they cannot keep long-term.

Figure 5.7. Competitors will work hard to undermine your stories. Make them resistant!

fourth or fifth feature here that could be decisive and tip the scales back in your favor?

As you saw in this example and see as well in figure 5.7, your competitor will engage in mudslinging. They will tell their own story about you, and they will make promises they can't keep. So you may have to train the customer to appreciate your differentiation as well. Dollars have a strong voice. Maybe you can show that the incremental costs of training and driver wages are still far less than the revenue they would forgo if they chose your competitors. You have to work hard to break down and change the customer perception.

This is something I'm religious about. You have to control your message! You have to be bolder in projecting in front of your customers. You can disagree respectfully, but then you need to show them the evidence. You have to project your perceptions religiously through value communication and tell the customers why you are different. Buyers are professionally trained—and in some cases rewarded—to generalize and neutralize and refuse to hear your differentiation, as figure 5.8 explains.

In the same vein, they are trained to bring up your bad points. If your message is weak or unsubstantiated, you are not only outnumbered in these negotiations. You are outgunned. Imagine if the business above wasn't a medium-sized business with three

- Break the team's *confidence* in their differentiation.
- Place you in a *commodity* bucket and focus on price.
- *Generalize* your positioning: "it is all the same."
- *Object* about your intended differentiation and *refuse* to hear about it during value and pricing discussions.
- Tell you what *stories* they hear about you in the market.
- Make lists of all your performance *breakdowns*, issues, and areas where your premium is not justified.

Figure 5.8. Professional buyers are trained to do this to you.

small warehouses but a leading national manufacturer with twenty large ones. What makes them different? Do they belong to a different segment, and do you face different competitors? Perhaps this large account is far beyond the ability of your other competitor to service. This customer wants to work with one lift-machine supplier, so this is an extremely lucrative key account. As I said at the beginning of this chapter, you need to be able to speak fluently in the dollars-and-cents language of value, and you need to be able to speak that language in this customer's dialect.

The thinking I outlined in this chapter needs to become a habit. You need frequent and continual validation with customers that you are delivering on the value you promised. You must train your commercial sales team and marketers on your own differentiation, so that they own it.

As simple as this process sounds, it is a surprisingly tough thing for people to do: Who are and *aren't* our customers? Why are we different? Finding the tough answers to these simple questions helps people stay focused. Get this down up front. If you put this into perspective, you can develop a value proposition versus competitors for each customer segment. As you go further in this book, you will sharpen this value proposition and quantify it in greater detail than I have described above, which was more back-of-the-envelope to whet your appetite and make a point. You have extracted benefits, understood them, and done apples-to-apples competitive analysis.

This process has to be a priority, because your market is dynamic. Customer needs and competitive capabilities are always in flux, even if short-term changes may seem slight. Keep doing your VRIO. Make it a habit. What you help people do with this approach is to find shared answers to simple business questions that every business person must know the answer to.

At this point, if you put these first five chapters into practice, your team can give you consistent and confident answers to questions about what your company does and why it adds value. It already keeps you honest. Let's say you have six sales calls today. Look at these questions for each call: What are our differentiators? How will I save these customers money or grow their revenue? What makes us unique and unstoppable?

Some things to keep in mind

1 **It is your responsibility to find your differentiation and make sure everyone in your organization is aligned on it.** Then you also have to message your differentiation systematically to the market to regain the upper hand in the "messaging war" and rebalance perceptions in the minds of your accounts. Ask your communication experts for help.

2 **Extracting true differentiation is not easy.** It requires a clear, proven approach and multifunctional work. Use the workshop format and conduct brainstorming sessions to go through the process of finding your true differentiation. Do this multiple times with multiple groups of internal folks. Then go outside and validate the outcome with customers. You will be surprised!

3   **Differentiation can be obvious or hidden, positive or negative, true or superficial, intended or perceived.** So you must look for it everywhere and pay attention to it. Marketing and strategic teams should know some of these already. It is best, however, to conduct the exercise nonetheless, because advantages are often transient. They are not static. Depending on how dynamic your market is, an exercise done six months ago may already be obsolete.

4   **My previous research shows that when internal folks know and believe in differentiation, they feel more confident about pricing in general.** In fact, it is one of the major drivers of pricing confidence. So do not underestimate the power of getting people re-energized about the level of true differentiation you have in your business. You will have to make it visible, train people on it, and communicate it widely. That work is ongoing, and it never ends.

5   **If you do not have great levels of established differentiation, do not stop looking.** Find the nuggets of differentiation and start with those. Then reinforce the fact that the business should focus on developing more differentiated products, services, and solutions through innovation.

Even if you stop reading this book now, you are in great shape! Take a breather and think about this final point. Most people who try to sell you on VBP would start their work where the next chapter in this book begins. Seriously! Think how impossible it would be to have started with chapter 6—and do steps 4 through 6 in the VBP process—if you hadn't done steps 1 through 3, as we just have.

Even better, nothing we have done so far has to do with the strategies, tactics, and mechanics of pricing! The truth is that you can't start a serious and fruitful discussion about pricing unless you have a firm and flexible grasp of differentiated value. Without that foundation, it is a dangerous waste of time.

You have your foundation in customer value (competition, segmentation, differentiation). Keep asking the questions to preserve it, and keep it current as we move on to the next steps.

Quantify Your Differentiation Value (Step 4)

VALUE IS A NUMBER. *Everything else is just noise. Over the first three steps of the value-based pricing (VBP) journey, you have collected and connected a large amount of information. You have learned a lot about the companies you compete with and, in some cases, the internal, do-it-yourself processes that your innovative solutions compete with. In other cases, you even compete against yourself when you launch the next generation of your products and services. You learned a lot about your customers and how to group them based on their needs rather than old-fashioned categorizations such as size or geography.*

In the last chapter you saw how to translate the features of your products and services into benefits, which are the counterparts to your customers' needs and the things they actually purchase from you. Finally, in rudimentary form, you saw how to convert those benefits into dollars, the language of value, relative to what your competitors provide. You learned to measure and express your differentiated value in a way that the customer understands and the competitor can't undermine.

Once you take this step, the noise stops. You are on the verge of having a message that cuts through the noise and hits home with customers, because they understand without ambiguity or guesswork just how much you can contribute to their financial and commercial success.

In this chapter we will go through that value modeling process in more detail, step by step. The EVE methodology (Economic Value Estimation) lies at the core of this process. By the time you have finished this chapter, you will have a more thorough understanding of how to express value in dollars, so that you can begin to make the most intelligent and best-informed pricing decisions you have ever made.

Economic Value Methodology (EVE) begins with customer benefits

Before we even get to the customer benefits in detail, I need to repeat a message you've heard many times already. Value is relative and not an absolute. Unless you have radical disruptive innovation and no reference value, what matters when you sell to your customers is not how much value you deliver, but how much *more* value do you bring versus the competition. This differential represents your true value, your differentiated value, which becomes the basis for your pricing strategy and price setting.

Value is always a number in B2B. You need a rational story about how much value you bring to the customer and the relevant stakeholders, and that rational story must include dollars. Saying you have 20 percent more reliability than competitors is a nice benefit, but that benefit closes sales only when you express it in terms of cost savings, revenue potential, or an emotional benefit, as shown in the value triad in figure 6.1.

The language in figure 6.1 is plain and straightforward. You are reducing costs or providing savings. On the cost-reduction side, perhaps your product offers lower weight or greater efficiency. Perhaps the benefit you provide helps the customer grow their revenue, potentially by charging higher prices. You can also provide a benefit through an emotional contribution: reassurance, confidence, lower risk, better relationships.

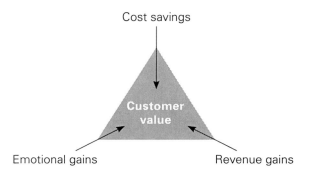

Figure 6.1. The value triad describes benefits from the customers' perspectives.

The value triad also shows where total cost of ownership (TCO) differs from VBP. TCO is focused on cost improvement. The customers can improve their margins only one way with that. The other way for your customers to improve margins is higher revenues through higher prices. In this case, you have enhanced the value of your customer's products to such an extent that they now have higher differentiated value. TCO is evolving into a concept called TBO, or total benefits of ownership, which encompasses savings and gains. VBP is still different from TBO, though, because it takes into account the emotional component (e.g., intangible benefits).

When a discussion begins about turning benefits into money, someone will inevitably use the word monetization. I need to make an important distinction here between monetization and dollarization. Many people use the terms interchangeably, but they're distinct, as I show in figure 6.2. Monetization can mean many things, from turning something illiquid into something liquid to any number of methods for converting an asset into money.

Monetization is the conversion of something into a stream of something else. It is a very general term. Dollarization is much more precise. You translate something specific (a customer benefit) into its equivalent impact in dollars and cents. It expresses in

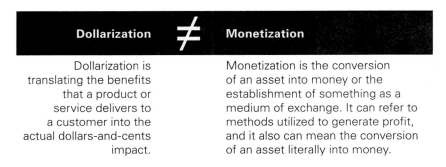

Dollarization $\neq$	Monetization
Dollarization is translating the benefits that a product or service delivers to a customer into the actual dollars-and-cents impact.	Monetization is the conversion of an asset into money or the establishment of something as a medium of exchange. It can refer to methods utilized to generate profit, and it also can mean the conversion of an asset literally into money.

Figure 6.2. The important difference between dollarization and monetization.

monetary terms the extent to which your products and services improve a customer's situation.

Monetization is only about creating the revenue stream regardless of the method you use to set prices or create it. Dollarization has more to do with value. This is a big difference and an important distinction. There is a telling comment about this in the movie *The Social Network,* when the Mark Zuckerberg character challenges his friend when the friend says they need to start monetizing the website.

"I know what the term means," he says, referring to monetization. "But what does that *mean*?"

Dollarization goes much further in depth than monetization. Dollarization forces you to create hard facts. The secret to dollarization is translating an attribute or product feature into a benefit, then creating a fact or a ratio or a number that reflects how you can change it or improve it. Let's say that figure is a 20 percent improvement in efficiency. Dollarization, as you saw in a basic way in the previous chapter, turns that 20 percent efficiency improvement into $1 million. That is the progression you need to think of. I realize it is hard work. I have encountered many companies that don't even express benefits in the first place, never mind finding a metric for them and then dollarizing them.

Building a value story based on hard facts

To have a rational conversation with B2B buyers, you need to create facts and show more numbers. But you can't drown or numb the buyers with your numbers. You have to wow them. When you translate your features into benefits and then into dollars, you have to keep priorities in mind. What will create that "wow" effect in the mind of buyers? What will make them sit up and pay closer attention?

You will have only limited time and limited space to tell your value story, so you have to lead with facts and numbers that will have the most dramatic impact. Your first value driver has to be your hook. This is true differentiation, not the nice-to-have category. You are superior here.

The first thing is to look at is how the customer talks. What units do they naturally or intuitively think in? If they are purchasing tires, do they think of value per tire, value per set of tires for the car, or lifetime value based on how long they last? This is how the customer understands products or product features. The same thinking applies to engines, as I show in figure 6.3.

Part of understanding your customers, as we saw in chapter 4, is listening closely to how they talk. You have to find a metric that is part of their day-to-day vocabulary. How do *they* think in terms of language and units? Do they think in terms of transactions, or do they think in terms of annual cycle or lifetime cycle when they perceive the value of what they buy? I know from experience that this decision takes some work. There are so many breakdowns at that level, so your best option is not always clear cut.

The right unit of measure up front: Use the value metric in the mind and vocabulary of the customer in their daily life.

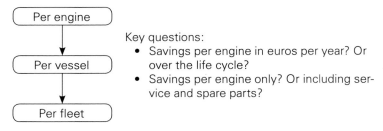

Key questions:
- Savings per engine in euros per year? Or over the life cycle?
- Savings per engine only? Or including service and spare parts?

Figure 6.3. Your unit of measure must reflect the way customers think and talk.

The next step is to translate these features into benefits. This is the next iteration in developing hypotheses about customer value and what your own differentiated value is. Typically an engineering-oriented company struggles with this step. Let's think about industrial gloves. From a cost and manufacturing standpoint, the engineers will say that there is no difference between a blue glove and a yellow glove. But the customer knows that yellow gloves are more recognizable, and studies have shown that assembly-line workers perceive yellow ones to be safer and more resilient than blue ones. These are real benefits in the eyes of the customer. Figure 6.4 lists some fundamental questions to ask as you think about how to translate features into benefits. You move from a product focus ("what do I offer?") to a benefit focus ("why should the customer care?") and ultimately to a value focus ("how much is it worth?").

I usually spend quite a bit of time on this. When I coach a team, I take their own materials and go through their own spec sheets to translate features into benefits. Let's say you have half a dozen differentiators. These are your value drivers. You need to name each value driver and then create a logic or a formula to express

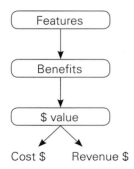

The process for hypothesizing economic value:
- **Product focus:** What do we offer?
- **Customer focus:** Why should the customer care?
- **Economic focus:** How much is that worth?

Figure 6.4. Key questions to ask as you move from features to benefits to value

that value in dollars and cents. The next step is to feed the formula. You need to find the data sources to make the calculations. You can do this with logic and back-of-the-envelope math, but I strongly encourage you to find independent empirical data. If you use government or other third-party data for this, you strengthen your case when converting the benefit into actual dollars.

Finally, you need to develop a value message that customers will find attractive and compelling. Figure 6.5 summarizes this process. This is what I meant by going from qualitative data and information to a solid quantitative basis that can underpin your rational selling arguments. You turn customer words into numbers and then into dollars. And believe me, everything can be dollarized.

I don't accept excuses that a business is so complex or so full of "soft" benefits that it defies dollarization. Services can also be dollarized. Intangibles can be dollarized. You can use techniques such as regression on satisfaction surveys, conjoint analysis, or Kano's model. If what you offer helps a customer make supply

Element	Example	Goal
Name/ description	Reduce warehouse operating cost	
Formula/ logic	warehouse workers rates × warehousing hours × percent improvement = reduction in warehouse labor costs	Quantify economically how we are better than the competition
Data/ source	$50 per hour × 24 hours a day × 10% daily improvement = $120 per day reduction in warehouse labor costs	
Message	Our superior solution will allow you to reduce the amount of time workers spend in the warehouse	

Figure 6.5. The process of taking your value drivers from definition to strong value message.

Customer words	Numbers	Dollarization
Yield improvement	40 grams per batch	40 grams × $100 per gram = $4,000 per batch
Reduced downtime	30 minutes of unplanned downtime per shift	30 minutes × $500 per minute = $15,000 per shift
Improved quality	100 units more first quality products to sell	100 units × $10 per unit = $1,000 per batch
Improved productivity	8 more units per hour	8 units × $10 per unit = $80 per hour
Better performance	3% gain in market share for customer	3 share points × $500,000 per point = $1.5 million

Figure 6.6. Quantifying and dollarizing benefits for products. You can dollarize anything. No excuses!

chain changes, or if you provide onsite support or training, that has a material impact for the customer that you can measure in dollars. Figure 6.6 shows some examples of how you can take rather general customer words and turn them into hard dollar amounts that you can compare directly—apples to apples—with what your competitors do. I recommend that you make the effort and use the ratio as a bridge between feature and dollars.

You should have no more than three to five value drivers that you can deliver against and that play an important role in your customer's business. Please keep in mind that the importance of the value drivers—and in some cases, the language they use to describe them—can vary by customer segment. Especially when we get down to this level, you should avoid making one-size-fits-all generalizations.

You might find what I say controversial. I do believe that everything can be translated into a number. I am not saying that you should use that number for everything. These are two distinct things: dollarizing differentiation value drivers and then projecting value through customer value propositions. It is clear that some customers do not need to hear a value proposition with fifteen dollarized items. Sometimes one is enough to win the customer over. If you are selling to end consumers, some dollarized numbers might feel awkward, so you need to be judicious in how many you choose and which ones.

Economic Value Methodology (EVE): The overall framework

As I mentioned in the previous chapter, you have to set aside your rose-colored glasses when you assess your value relative to your competitors. There will almost invariably be cases where you have negative value drivers. Perhaps customers have a longer ramp-up time with your products and services, or perhaps they are more training-intensive. You need to make sure you take these negatives into account as well. Be candid when you do this exercise. You can't be the best or equal everywhere.

This is yet another reason why you need to know your competitors better than they know themselves. You need to do the most thorough and most honest job of estimating your value. Figure 6.7 explains how to take this negative differentiation value into account. This is based on work done by Monitor Group. The difference between your positive and negative value differentiation is a surplus that I refer to as the value pool. In this case the value is the difference between what you provide and what your reference competitor offers.

People usually understand this point about the value pool. I always remind people that although this process is a numbers-driven science, it is also an art. There is no single right answer to selling value. Instead, you need to find *your* right answer, the one that works for your market, your customers, and

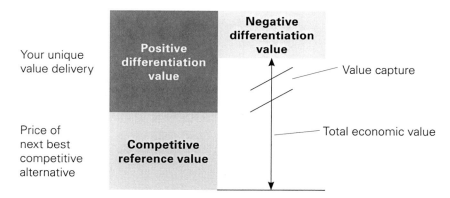

Figure 6.7. Economic Value Estimation framework: The basic framework for determining your value pool.

your organization. You need to find your own secret sauce, and you need to gather perspectives from multiple functions. Just as there is no single right answer, there is no one in your organization who has a monopoly on how your customers think and how much value you add. Having these checks and balances is healthy.

Economic Value Methodology (EVE): How to get started

The first challenge, again, is to figure out the mental frames that your customers (end users, OEMs, distributors) use when they think about your products or services. These lead to your value drivers, and you should have at least three but normally no more than five. Having too few gives you less flexibility in negotiations (fewer levers) and may also indicate that you don't completely understand the customer's business and its complexity. Having too many will muddy your story and blunt the impact of your most important arguments. It may also indicate that you don't understand your customer's business because you can't distinguish with confidence what truly matters to them and what is mere noise. This step is crucial, because customer value modeling culminates in a value story or value script, as I show in the process in figure 6.8.

Once you have set priorities, you need to think about how to build your value story. What drivers do you start with? I recommend focusing on the biggest bang or the most compelling hook and concluding with a strong value proposition in terms of dollars-and-cents impact. There is a psychological motivation behind this known as the primacy and latency effects. People tend to remember the first and last things they hear better than the story in the middle, and also to give those outer factors more weight. You should take advantage of these thought patterns.

When people struggle with these steps, the most common root cause I notice is that they have made their models too complicated. Take a close look at the value drivers you have chosen and their associated impacts. Do you really need to put the tiny marginal savings there? Just because you have created a value model and a value story doesn't mean that the craft of sales and selling has fallen by the wayside. You use the first two drivers to sell them and hook them; then you can switch to a customer conversation. The worst thing you can do is become robotic and slavishly go

1 *Translate* differentiators into customer benefits (using customer vocabulary, thinking process, mental frames).
2 *Prioritize* customer benefits based on segment (most compelling hook and last impression).
3 Turn these benefits into compelling *facts* and ratios (% faster, increase of 2 pts of yield, 1/3 more durability).
4 *Dollarize* these benefits into $, £, ¥ or € (dramatic numbers, round numbers, compelling savings/gains).
5 Create your *value story* or value script.

Figure 6.8. The overall approach to customer value modeling.

"Okay, now let's look at value driver #7." You need communication, not recitation.

Storytelling is essential to making sure customers understand and embrace your story. Even the strongest numbers can't speak for themselves. Use the ratios and then the dollars so that the logic is transparent and intuitive for the customer. Use dramatic, round numbers and skip the decimal points. Your arguments need to be robust, but too much detail is a clear distraction when you are telling a story. That is why this task requires some emotional intelligence as well. If you have too much value, or fail to engage the customer in a conversation, you can lose credibility.

B2B and industrial teams usually get the middle part of the list, the supporting cast of drivers. It is harder for them to pick out the stars in your value proposition, stand behind them, and make them shine bright. Their passion and inclination for objectivity makes it hard for them to tell a story that is compelling, and is why such a story is necessary. This process will always be a mixture of science (objectivity) and art (subjectivity). Figure 6.9 shows the ten steps I use to make an EVE model.

You need a context for the model first: who is it for, what products, what function, and so forth. This forces you to remember—

1 *Contextualize* your value model: segment, region, function, etc.
2 *List* differentiators/value drivers (tangible/intangible).
3 Select the most *relevant* value drivers.
4 Translate them into *customer benefits*.
5 Create the value *formula* and relevant variables.
6 *Measure* value of the relevant variables.
7 Calculate *total* economic value and value pool.
8 Identify the relevant pricing *moderators*.
9 Create value *messages* for each driver.
10 Design the *value proposition* or value story.

Figure 6.9. The ten steps of customer value modeling.

once again—that value is both segment-specific and relative to the competition. Always! It can also vary by country. Yes, the conclusion you probably just came to is correct. You may ultimately have hundreds of value models. This is an additional powerful incentive to keep your models clean and simple. They should always focus on the most compelling essential arguments.

This plea for simplicity and focus is a common thread throughout this book. Don't overcomplicate the process and overthink it, because you will do this exercise so often. You also have to have the rigor, discipline, and patience to brainstorm again and again. Don't assume that you already know all the value drivers well. Look at all tangible and intangible benefits as you try to list differentiators and value drivers. Ask yourself whether what you are doing today is the right approach. When you have the finance and the tech and the quality people together in the same room, they will all tell you different things. So include some soft factors, as well, and get all the different perspectives.

After the first pass with a large, cross-functional team, you may have a dozen drivers on your brainstorming list. From that dozen, you may conclude that six are legitimate, meaning they matter deeply to the customers in that segment. But then you still need to narrow that list even further, looking not only at relevance and customer focus but also at credibility, whether you can measure it and whether you can quantify its value. If I am moderating this exercise, I force the group to get under five drivers, and I always aim for three whenever possible. In my view, any value proposition with more than three dollarized messages is too much. It means you haven't done your evaluation the right way. But I also recognize that not everyone can get to this gold standard, at least on the first few tries. That is why I can sometimes accept value propositions with four or at most five drivers. For each driver, you need to create a value message and a story. The more people you have from different functions, the more help you can get with a story. In the end, remember that one driver might do the job. The simpler the better. Keep in mind the buyer or customer in front of you.

To define and assess the value pool, you need to look at your net differentiation value and your reference value. You will also need to think about how to share this value pool. Setting prices in a way that gives you the entire value pool means that the customer derives no net benefit from what you offer. Conceding the entire value pool to the customer means that *you* achieve no advantage from the value you create. Capturing value—which will we look at in detail in subsequent chapters—means finding the right middle ground. Once you know the size of the value pool, you will have to decide how much of it you want to capture. How much of the pool can you capture in a bid? What are your price moderators, the mitigating factors that can also be positive or negative?

The process described in figure 6.9 seems like a lot of steps. This is a progression and not a menu. I see engineers eager to skip straight to the calculations, even though they can't yet be sure that the numbers they come up with mean anything or express anything that matters in the day-to-day lives of customers. You can't omit any steps! At the same time, you shouldn't get intimidated or discouraged. This process will become natural and intuitive after a while, especially when you see the benefits and start to reap them.

Beyond the ten steps, there are some other things you must do when you are modeling value. You will find these in figure 6.10. It is important to contextualize your model. Be aware of who the model is for and how you can apply it. This prevents you from getting swept up in the details and falling in love with your own work. You also need to keep careful track of your assumptions and hypotheses, not only to preserve the whole picture and context of

- *Contextualize* your model.
- List all *assumptions* and hypotheses.
- Document your *calculations*.
- Document your data *sources*.
- Keep track of the model *version*.

Figure 6.10. Several must-do items when you model customer value.

the model but also to monitor them and perhaps adjust them as you get new information.

The quality of your data and your assumptions will affect your individual and collective confidence, which will manifest itself when you are presenting your value stories and negotiating with customers. So you also need to document your calculations. Everyone needs to see and understand what's behind the calculations and assumptions. You also need to document your data sources. Personnel can change as people take on new roles and new people enter the organization. The better you document your data sources, the easier these people can get up to speed on the basis of your model and the answers you have derived. You can even make citations in your value documents. The more you use a range of data sources, the more credible your data model will be. Finally, you need to avoid the curse of modern collaboration, which often spans regions and time zones: version confusion! You need to make sure at all times that you have the latest, most up-to-date version. This can be difficult, but the investment is worth it. The work involved in undoing a situation when you have multiple versions is very frustrating and can also damage trust you have built up within your team.

I have already touched on many of the points in figure 6.11, where I highlight the key success factors in value modeling. In my experience, one of the most important points is to assemble the right team and err on the side of casting a wider net rather than a tighter one. Include human resources, IT, and operations. Don't

- *Contextualized* activity as part of value programs.
- Dedicated *brainstorming* sessions.
- *Cross-functional* teams: sales, marketing, pricing, finance, quality, technical, operations, HR, etc.
- *Practical* and well-prepared exercises.
- *Variety* of exercises: innovations, core products, services, systems, software, etc.
- Focus on *efforts* and progress, not on perfect outcome (both a science and an art).
- Focus on *iterative process*, not on 100% precision.
- 50% training + 50% practice = 100% *fun*.

Figure 6.11. The key success factors in value modeling.

do this exercise alone or in isolation! It must be part of a wider value activity. You need to remind people why you have undertaken this effort. You need to brainstorm in a meaningful way. I highly recommend that you conduct the brainstorming sessions offsite. Throw away the key, put people in a room in groups of five or six each, and leave the laptops behind. This exercise is too vital to walk through or to undertake casually. If you try to do it in the office, people will escape during the breaks and may never return. You need them to immerse in the customer experience.

When you do this work, use your own real products. I don't train on widgets. This is also important for change management, because you need to see in your own context that this work is not only doable but desirable. For your first effort, pick a range of products, from new ones to established ones, and from stand-alone products to bundled solutions. Let each group share its work, so that you can see the differences, check assumptions, and allow some room for error.

Finally, as I have said in other contexts before, focus on effort and celebrate progress instead of going after a perfect outcome. The very first time you go through the gymnastics of your customers' daily lives (by segment, of course), the process will take some time. Nonetheless, you need to have a positive experience with these sessions. The first activities have to be successful, be fun, and create buzz in the organization, so that other people will want to do it too. One reason why I certify is that people pay attention. But once you have put in the initial effort and gained some experience, each session gets shorter. It's like riding a bike, and at some point you can ride hands-free without a helmet—but be careful. You will eventually see convergence and realize that you have achieved an optimal outcome, meaning the incremental gains from going further do not justify the incremental effort.

Where do you get the data?

Data is the fuel that powers your models. Figure 6.12 is an overview of the many ways you get hard data or at least make solid assumptions. As I said earlier when we looked at competitive and customer data, you have to triangulate. This means using multiple techniques and multiple sources, because no one method, on its own, will give you the right answer. Put another way: one method, in isolation, will give you a wrong answer. You have to triangulate. This is a mindset shift, but it's a necessity. Data gathering and data analysis can create a mess of complexity and controversy. They require a lot of skill, especially when you are interviewing

- **Industry associations**: reports, trends, etc.
- **Consultants and research organizations**: industry surveys, cost surveys, omnibus surveys, customer surveys, etc.
- **Independent experts**: retired employees, specialists, etc.
- **Specialized data companies**: International Data Group (IDG)
- **Competitors**: websites, product data sheets, application data sheets
- **Third-party labs and technical centers**: data warehouses and data banks
- **Government and academic institutions**: official economic data
- **Noncompeting enterprises**: pooled research efforts and shared data

Figure 6.12. Critical sources of value data.

customers in the field. Some methods are more reliable than others, and all have their peculiar strengths and weaknesses.

Remember that you have to understand the value you deliver—benefit by benefit—from two perspectives: what you deliver to the customer, and what your competitors deliver to the customer. The difference (hopefully positive!) is your net differentiated value. The sources in figure 6.12 primarily give you data on your competitors' capabilities, and perhaps insights into what matters to your customers and to what degree. Many of these sources are generally accepted as valid, especially data from governments, academic research, or reputable associations. Some of these tests have thousands of observations behind them. Amazon reviews are similar and have broadened into the B2B realm. You can also buy or find data or hire independent experts or retired employees. They can give you KPIs, help you with the customer language, and give you insights into how the customers think and how they make decisions. You can also look at noncompeting enterprises and exchange data, which often results in a mutually beneficial relationship.

You have to be proactive to make sure you have the right data and even challenge the findings rather than take things at face value. Much is riding on the value model, so the data must be as strong as possible. Something you do (a service, a product feature) could be a value destroyer just as much as a value creator.

But you will notice that the word "customer" appears only once in figure 6.12. There are other ways to get additional indirect as well as direct input from customers that you can use in your value modeling. These sources are summarized in figure 6.13. The table includes direct and indirect approaches to customer research. I appreciate that even to this day, some people have a bias against customer research. They may even quote Henry Ford, who once claimed that if he asked customers what they wanted, they wouldn't

Value assessment method	Method complexity	Overall reliability	Ease of execution	Internal skills requirements	Critical success factors
Internal engineering assessment	+++	+++	+	+++	Test method design and repeatability
Field value-in-use assessment	+++	+++	+	+++	Customer access and cooperation
Indirect survey questions	++	+	+++	+	Interviewing skills with decision makers
Focus group value assessment	+	+	+++	+	Group dynamics and participation
Direct survey questions	++	+	+++	++	Interviewing skills with decision makers
Conjoint or tradeoff analysis	+++	++	+	+++	Sampling method and good data
Benchmarks	+	+	++	+	Willingness of respondents to give reliable and transparent value information
Compositional approach	+	++	++	++	Willingness of respondents to give reliable and transparent value information
Importance ratings	++	+	++	+	Focus on importance of value drivers

Figure 6.13. There is no shortage of sources for data on customer value; each has its strengths and weaknesses.

have said they wanted cars. They would have wanted faster horses. Nonetheless, these approaches do yield useful insights into the perceived value customers have, as long as you keep in mind that you have to triangulate instead of relying exclusively or heavily on one source or method.

I would like to take a more in-depth look at two of these approaches: the value-in-use assessment and the internal engineering assessment. The value-in-use work can be insightful, but it requires a team from your side whose members are extremely inquisitive and observant, and who pay great attention to detail. To the greatest extent possible, they will immerse themselves in a "day in the life" of the customer.

They will need to map the customer's applications and make flowcharts and blueprints of their processes (see figure 6.14). From beginning to end, they need to take notes, count the seconds, observe the handoffs, and so on. The best people today for this work are applications engineers. Once you have their process maps, you can validate the points and ask additional questions through internal discussions at the customer. This process will give you the most precise understanding of what you can improve in the customers' processes and of what that improvement might

1 Understand and map *customer applications* and production process.
2 Break down *customer process* using value engineering flowcharts, process maps, and blueprints.
3 Conduct a *day in the life of a customer* session to identify potential areas of pains or gains.
4 Conduct *site observations* (ethnographic research): takes notes, photos, flowcharts, time measures, and others.
5 Validate findings with *direct interviews* of experts in the product, quality and engineering departments to refine time, materials and process analyses.
6 Assemble multi-functional team to elaborate *value-in-use reports*.

Figure 6.14. Approaches to conducting value-in-use analysis.

be worth to them. In your follow-up discussions with internal experts, you can bring money into the conversation and map the money against the processes. The customer spends X on one part of the process. Is that normal? Is that an exception? What's the rule? You can never ask these question without having observed the processes "live" first.

Reverse-engineering can also be a great source of data, but it is just as demanding in its own way as value-in-use assessments. In this case, you try to replicate a customer's production process in your own lab. The difference in perspective here, in contrast to the value-in-use, is that you are recreating the production processes rather than merely observing them. I summarize some of the key points for engineering assessments in figure 6.15. As much as I would love to elaborate on each of these in-depth but insightful approaches, I have to defer. Like competitive analysis and customer segmentation, these approaches warrant a book unto themselves.

So what does the output look like?

If you are fortunate, you will have positive total net differentiation value. As I have implied a few times in this chapter and in the

1 *Reverse engineer* customer applications and products.
2 *Duplicate* customer production process in your lab with mini-plant and testing equipment.
3 Conduct internal *tests* in applications: ASTM, USCar tests, etc.
4 Validate internal tests and measurements by external third-party labs that are widely recognized.
5 *Validate* your engineering *assumptions* early in the process in the relevant industry community.
6 Use widely recognized engineering *methodologies*. Develop new ones when needed using best-in-class institutions.

Figure 6.15. Steps to conducting an engineering assessment.

previous one, no one is perfect, and you can't be superior in everything. By definition, when someone is better, it means someone else is worse. And there are situations when you are that worse firm. In other cases, you may have zero differentiation value, which means you may need to use intangibles to defend your premium or define your minimum.

No one likes to talk about these situations, which obviously must be common: a competitor is indeed superior to you. This can be a shock sometimes. We think we have differentiation, but maybe we have lost market leadership? If that happens, admit it. You may perform on certain features, if not many features, below your reference value. In such cases, you have to flip the rationale for the model around. Instead of looking for a premium you can justify, you need to explain the basis for the discount you give. Your goal is to limit the discounts you offer while still conducting the negotiations on a rational basis. The customer value model helps you define and explain the negative gap between you and your reference competition in a way that is clear and defensible. This prevents you from getting beaten up on price. You can be honest, but you can also sell the future and inform the customers how you plan to eliminate these performance gaps. Figure 6.16 shows the possible outcomes of customer value modeling.

Your ideal case is case 1 in the figure. The stack on the left shows the accumulation of value from all the ways you have a positive differentiation. The dark block is the negative differentiation representing the dollar value of the areas where your competitors are superior. The remainder, the large bar on the right side of case 1, is your value pool.

In case 2, the positives offset the negatives, leaving you with zero net differentiated value. In this case you need to tap into your intangibles (brand, risk minimization, trust) and defend your price points. In case 3, the model has flipped. You have a net

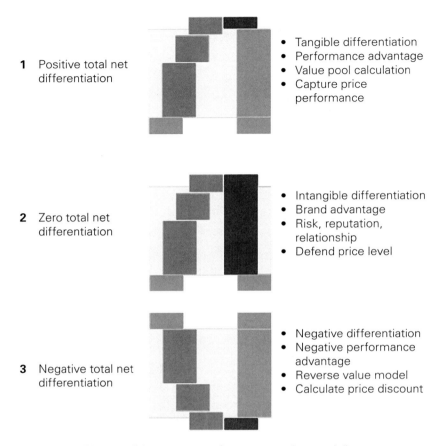

1 Positive total net differentiation

- Tangible differentiation
- Performance advantage
- Value pool calculation
- Capture price performance

2 Zero total net differentiation

- Intangible differentiation
- Brand advantage
- Risk, reputation, relationship
- Defend price level

3 Negative total net differentiation

- Negative differentiation
- Negative performance advantage
- Reverse value model
- Calculate price discount

Figure 6.16. The possible outcomes of customer value modeling.

negative differentiation, and you need to use that as a basis for deriving an appropriate, rational discount.

No matter the outcome, the message here is that you need to take control of your own destiny. The value numbers, expressed in dollars, empower you to do this. You need to know the size of your value pool, regardless of how you decide to set your prices later.

Figure 6.17 provides a closer look at one of these value stacks. It is the EVE for a heavy equipment manufacturer. You will notice

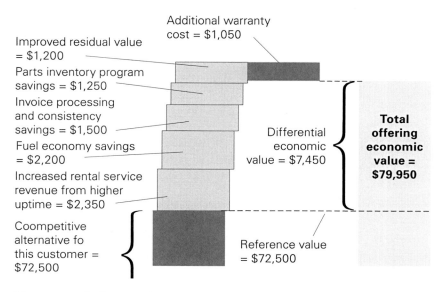

Additional warranty cost = $1,050

Improved residual value = $1,200

Parts inventory program savings = $1,250

Invoice processing and consistency savings = $1,500

Fuel economy savings = $2,200

Increased rental service revenue from higher uptime = $2,350

Coompetitive alternative fo this customer = $72,500

Differential economic value = $7,450

Reference value = $72,500

Total offering economic value = $79,950

Figure 6.17. EVE output for a heavy equipment manufacturer. Notice the mix of drivers, which provides the positive differentiated value.

that the company has a differential economic value of $7,450 over the competition. This differential comprises firm dollar amounts from five different drivers, which represent savings (e.g., fuel, parts) as well as an estimate of increased revenue due to the machines' longer uptimes. The only offset is the fact that the company's warranty is more expensive than the reference competitor's. This differential value of $7,450 represents the value pool. As we will see in the next chapter, this is the basis for value sharing and pricing decisions. Figure 6.17 also encapsulates the blueprint for your negotiations, by defining the drivers in customer language and quantifying them with some precision.

You are always fighting for either a higher price or a lower discount. Don't discount without knowing how much value you create or what your relative value is. You have to admit that it would have been impossible for you to develop a pricing and negotiation blueprint with this much relevance, flexibility, and precision without going through the process we have followed so far in this book. Your own experience and internal knowledge and expertise clearly informed all of this work, but on its own it would not have been sufficient without a process for channeling and quantifying it.

At the same time, I need to admit that doing all of these calculations is hard to manage over time, and across multiple products and customer segments, without some technological support. This is especially true if you work for a large, diversified company. There is no way a Fortune 500 company can do these things by hand. There is no way you can update them and keep the logic straight when you have too many customers or products. That is why I recommend that you adopt some kind of technology, not just to accelerate the systematic use but also to maintain version control and allow more people to get involved in the process. Figure 6.18 shows an example of this software, from a company called

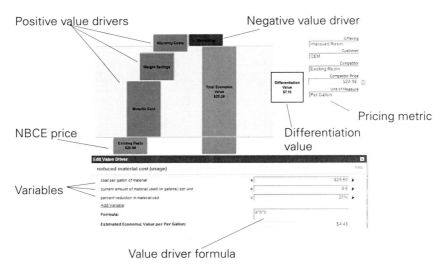

Figure 6.18. The EVE software provided by LeveragePoint Innovations.

LeveragePoint Innovations. This software is currently in use in many companies that are known to be value masters. Make no mistake. If you are managing thousands of SKUs with thousands of marketing, pricing, and sales professionals, it will be difficult to calculate VBP by hand or in Excel. In fact, it would take you years to get there, and most likely you would make many mistakes— visible and invisible—along the way. Value and sales enablement software allows for:

- documentation of previous work
- the integrated management of a library of value drivers that can be reused and shared
- the acceleration of the production of dollarized customer value propositions that can be pushed to the salesforce automatically
- faster feedback from the market on the value-based price of your innovations.

Some things to keep in mind

1 **Before you begin dollarizing anything, make sure you have done the proper exercise for a specific segment and against a specific competitor.** This has to become very granular. It is why you might have to produce dozens or hundreds of EVE of customer value models. In one specific segment, you might have three subsegments and six competitors and maybe five main countries. You do the arithmetic!

2 **Dollarization is a science and a process.** You have to learn the mechanics and get the data. That part is the easy part. Going from dollarization to crafting customer value propositions for customer-facing interactions is something else entirely. You need to know the art of storytelling. So you

get the point! It is a combination of art and science. We don't want to turn our sales reps into robots that project nothing but numbers day-in and day-out. We want to adapt the customer value proposition and the numbers to the customer the sales reps have in front of them.

3 **It is better to be roughly right than precisely wrong.** Sometimes, we search too much for the exact number. Do we need to be 100 percent right on the number? Of course not. I often recommend finding a number that is credible and proposing a range in front of the customer. We want to find credible numbers that will not send the customer running or create an adverse reaction.

4 **In the end, focus on the overall story line.** Use the value drivers that are the most customer-centric and project one or two critical messages. Round up the numbers. Then use the numbers as backup to discussing value. Be simple and compelling. That is the priority.

5 **Doing dollarization of differentiation is the heart of the VBP process.** While everything should be dollarized, not every dollar can or should be used with customers or end users. You will prepare several versions of your models for distributors, end users, customers, and others. The drivers will be different for your distributors, as the business model is different. You want to have more value conversations and fewer price negotiations.

You are now roughly halfway through the book, and only now can you start thinking confidently and specifically about pricing! How you set your prices is a function of how you want to share your value pool with customers. That is a strategic decision, but one that you cannot take properly without knowing the size of your value pool. The size of the value pool is one of the most important and insightful numbers your business has. And it is one you could never calculate in a rational, transparent, defensible way without the steps you have just taken.

7

Understand the Value Pool and Setting Prices (Steps 5 and 6)

THE VALUE POOL IS *a destination you have to reach. While I don't want to compare the value-based pricing (VBP) process with a tortuous trek across a desert, you can think of the value pool as the refreshing water at the oasis. "Value pool" is a concept you won't see prominently in pricing literature, but it can help you choose your business model, inform your pricing strategy, select your pricing metrics, set your price points, and engage your customers with value conversations.*

Having said that, I don't do the homework and all the math for you. I will stress again that this book is neither formulaic nor prescriptive. It is guidance, meant

to open eyes and show you a path to VBP that you can
actually navigate from beginning to end without getting
sidetracked, bogged down, lost, or frustrated. I am
showing you the map and where the roads lead across
the desert. You need to make the choices and undertake
the journey.

Value management: What the value pool is, and why it matters

You can't do VBP if you don't know the nature, size, and the stability of your value pool. The value pool is the amount of money available for exchange and sharing with your customers or distributors, in the form of prices. Without that knowledge, there is no way for you to set the right price for the value you deliver. This is not a criticism or indictment of your prevailing pricing practices, which are probably based on costs, competition, or a combination of the two. As I said in the opening chapter, I will not insult or belittle your previous practices, as many advocates of VBP are liable to do. You wouldn't be in business today with satisfied and/or repeat customers if you were not delivering value.

Leaving out pricing until now is not intuitive for people. You don't need to know pricing to understand value, but you need to understand value to find the prices that best fit your products, services, and strategic goals. Value management has three steps: creation, dollarization, and capture (see figure 7.1). These correspond to the deceptively simple questions I have asked throughout the book: What do you do for customers? What is it worth? How much of it will you capture? Only that last phase (capture) requires some knowledge of pricing.

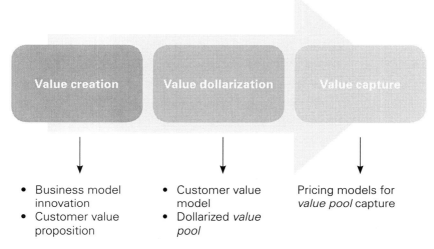

- Business model innovation
- Customer value proposition

- Customer value model
- Dollarized *value pool*

Pricing models for *value pool* capture

Figure 7.1. The three steps of value management. First measure the value, and then capture as much of it as possible.

If you are still in business and have made money, then you have been creating and capturing value all along. Knowing the size of your value pool is a way to measure how well your previous prices worked relative to your business strategy and your competitive advantages. Let's say that cost-based pricing or competition-based pricing has historically allowed you to capture 20 or 25 percent of a large value pool. You wouldn't know that or have any real clue about how well you are really doing unless you have done the work so far in this book. It would have been impossible for you to make such a statement until now. Armed with the more precise estimates of your value pool, you can conclude that yes, you have done reasonably well, but you also have tremendous *measurable* upside based on your differentiated value. Your current prices are too low. You could raise them and still remain competitive.

You may also have cases where you are capturing 80 to 90 percent of a small value pool, which could indicate that you are overpriced. Your current prices may be too high, and you would be more competitive if you reduced them selectively. Either way, you lack a rational, evidence-based foundation for taking a price increase or decrease until you know your value pool. It is just not possible. You can get close, and guesswork gets you in the area. But to get the right answer you need a value pool.

When you know your value pool, you sit in a powerful position rather than a vulnerable one. When you communicate your value story and set your prices, you know what you are giving away and what you are keeping. You are in fact in greater control of your destiny! You also seize the opportunity to train your audience—customers, investors, analysts, and the broader market—via long-term, consistent value communication. When you raise prices, your moves are reasonable because they take place within the same framework of a value division that your customers are familiar with. And when you use the value pool systematically, it makes it easier to raise your prices and to remind your customers and distributors that you are still delivering great value to them despite raising prices.

The value pool defines your price discretion, which lies between maximum ceiling and the floor (parity with your reference competitors). You need to establish your price-setting mechanism and decide how much you will capture. Well-known companies vary in this regard, depending on the industry and strategy. Companies such as Apple, Procter & Gamble, Starbucks, and Disney price high and take a lot of their value pools. 3M varies the amount it takes by industry segment.

What you have experienced over the first four steps in the VBP process is the fundamental difference between VBP and cost-based or competition-based pricing. The latter two approaches are the shortest paths to a price, and that is one big reason why people skip the value analysis and go as quickly as possible to setting a price. Most people want to jump right into pricing activities, because pricing is something they already do. They don't take a close look at the pains they solve and gains they make possible for customers. Some people skip the dollarization part as well. But the vast majority of the work in VBP involves getting to the value pool, which means understanding the most important customer benefits you provide and expressing them in dollar terms. When you have done that, you have all the data and assumptions and alignment you need. Finding the right price mechanism is easier, and you do so with more confidence.

Value capture and pricing mechanisms

Pricing is about sharing the value pool and optimizing the amount of money you capture. You can be creative here, within market circumstances and the constraints your starting point may impose on you. Let the amount of dollars and your desire to share drive your choice of a pricing mechanism, rather than choosing a mechanism beforehand and trying to force it to work. Figure 7.2 describes the kind of flexibility and constraints you may have.

BM and CVP that are
- Disruptive and differentiated
- Solution-oriented
- High customer WTP
- High value pool to share

} New pricing model to capture value using a *new* value metric as part of a *unique* profit formula (new pricing frame of reference versus competitors)

BM and CVP that are:
- Incremental and imitable
- Product-oriented
- In tradional sector
- low value pool to share

} New pricing model to capture value using an *existing* value metric as part of a *traditional* profit formula (premium versus competitors based on value)

Figure 7.2. Factors influencing pricing model generation. Your goals, circumstances, and the size of your value pool determine your flexibility.

Knowing the size of your value pool simplifies your choice of business model and pricing strategy. It also helps you revisit the strength of your customer value proposition (CVP). Instead of staring at a huge flowchart full of if-then statements to find your optimal pricing model, you can use the options in figure 7.2 as your guide. If you have a small value pool, you should share that value and stick with prevailing pricing metrics in your market. In that case, you are in the bottom half of figure 7.2. You don't have the power or leverage to change market dynamics.

If you have a large pool, the chances are high that there is a mismatch between the old pricing models and the size of the pool. In other words, if you have a lot of differentiation, lots of willingness-to-pay (WTP), and a correspondingly large pool, you can introduce a new value metric and change the industry's pricing formula. Two prominent examples of companies that did this are GE, with aircraft engines, and Michelin, with passenger and industrial vehicle tires.

At first glance, tires may seem to be more of a commodity product with little room for differentiation. Michelin discovered that there was so much money in its value pool that there was indeed a disconnect between the price-per-product approach and the depth of the value pool. Finding themselves in the area represented by the top half of figure 7.2, Michelin changed to a *distance-based* pricing model rather than a *unit-based* one. When the source of your value is reliability, durability, and longevity, a distance-based model is much better aligned with that value than a unit-based one is.

The value pool calculation in this context can become a game-changing exercise. I have seen dollarization exercises for services and software where the value pool calculation led to millions of dollars of savings for customers. Due to the efficiency gains offered to customers, the numbers were so large that they even lacked internal credibility and impacted the team's confidence. Faced with such high numbers, we were forced to revisit segmentation and our versioning strategy. If you go before a prospective customer and inform them that they can save millions with a $20,000 software package, for example, you might run into credibility issues and face value objections.

The documentation of the value pool is also critical. The best way to convince a customer of your value is to deliver on your promises. Historically, most companies have confirmed the delivery of value through solid but indirect indicators such as repeat business, customer satisfaction, and positive qualitative feedback. But we know now that value is multifaceted. Given its many aspects, it is almost impossible to track it holistically. In the spirit of the saying "what gets measured gets done," I recommend the use of scorecards, as shown in figure 7.3, to document and verify value, and to provide empirical evidence so that you can adjust and strengthen your value stories accordingly. These models need to be retrievable for use in a sales context. You can create and jointly manage the value pool together with your customers. This form of partnership makes the sharing transparent as well. That's the ideal situation, especially with value buyers across the table.

10 to 15 key dollarized differentiators:
- Product value
- Service value
- Software and technology
- Brand

Verified value measures:
- Value audit
- Six Sigma project
- Joint task force
- Technology (CRM)

Figure 7.3. Scorecards help you track value along each differentiator rather than holistically.

The scorecards also help you establish the idea of value creation and value quantification, so that even reluctant customers can get the idea and begin warming up to it. By controlling the discussion this way, you set the perceptions and parameters and have a much stronger case for price adjustments (if any) as economic conditions improve or worsen. Value scorecards are best used with strategic accounts and/or value buyers. They help encourage customers and distributors to hold quarterly value reviews or discussions. They force the discussion to focus on the holistic management of the value that is in fact delivered to them. The scorecards do not have to be complex or super sophisticated. I have seen them created simply in Excel or PowerPoint and managed manually. The key is not so much the way they are managed but rather the capacity of account managers to track and calculate the outcome of the value projects and activities. They require discipline in value homework and tracking efforts. Ideally and eventually, value scorecards ought to be managed in a powerful CRM software and automatically produced periodically. But that is at times wishful thinking!

Value adjustments: Moderating how much you should share

Our general sense of fairness reflexively tells us that a 50/50 split is ideal. But pricing decisions are more complex and require more subtlety than, say, cutting up an apple and sharing it with someone. The best price is the one the customer understands as a fair split against the value, and in a B2B market this may not always correspond to a 50/50 share of the value pool. The easiest way to appreciate that is to think of a highly innovative product that creates a large value pool. Buying that product improves the quality or cost position of the buyer's own products to such an extent that it would be at a disadvantage if it included a cheaper or less valuable alternative instead. In such a case, the supplier is justified in capturing more than 50 percent of the value pool.

I refer to these adjustments—both positive and negative—as moderators. These moderators should not be confused with the negative differentiators discussed earlier. Pricing moderators are used to establish price points between the reference value and the theoretical maximum price that customers should be willing to pay for the value they receive. They are included in the last step of the process. Negative differentiators are unique costs to your offering.

Figure 7.4 shows the route from differentiated value pool (total value available to share) to price (the amount of the pool you capture) via the use of moderators. They help you decide how to

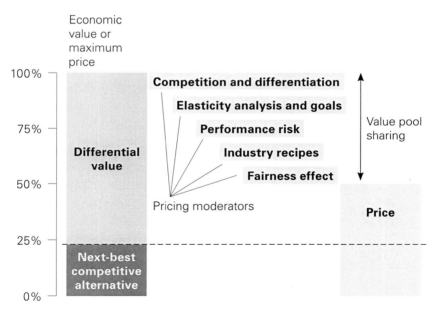

Figure 7.4. EVE and price setting. Pricing moderators take you step by step from value pool to value capture (price).

regulate the prices within the pool in a transparent and rational way. Let's look at the major categories individually.

Competition and differentiation. By definition, you would not have a large value pool without significant net differentiated value. However, your net value comprises many drivers where you have varying degrees of superiority or even inferiority. The more competitors that can exploit one of your weakness or disadvantages, and the size of that disadvantage, the more carefully you need to capture value. These drivers can become your Achilles' heel. In contrast, if you face little competition and have few weaknesses and one or two clearly dominant strengths, you have greater pricing leverage

Elasticity analysis. Many pricing consultants and academics see price elasticity as an indispensable, even deterministic factor in price setting. Economics 101 textbooks agree with them. I see price elasticity as a moderating factor, not a determining one. That is why you are seeing the phrase "price elasticity" for the very first time in this book. Price elasticity is a measure of price response and price sensitivity. It is defined as the ratio of the percentage change in volume to the percentage change in price. If small price changes cause big shifts in volume, you have high price elasticity. If large price changes elicit only small changes in volume, you have low price elasticity. Your customers are less sensitive to price. Use this information, if you have it, to adjust how much of the value pool you capture. But I advise against making a strict, functional link between price elasticity and the prices you charge.

Goals. What do you want? That frustratingly simple question encompasses your financial and commercial objectives. How do you balance revenue, volume, and profit? How important is market share to you? These goals can vary from product to product, even if you have an overarching, company-wide position that generally applies. Some products lend themselves to a penetration strategy so that you can build share, create awareness, and give a larger audience a chance to experience what it is like to work with you. Other products and services are meant to capitalize on that platform. For them, you may use a skimming approach, which means you take a higher share of the value pool; that is, you charge higher prices.

Performance risk. This is a very relevant consideration, as a series of recent high-profile cases have shown. They include the gypsum board from China and the ignition switches on cars from General Motors. These issues raise the question of whether you want to sell on fear: How forcefully do you want to use risk as a selling point and make customers aware of the major damage and in some cases the liabilities that can result when they accept lower value for a lower price? It is in your interest to document market failures and create stories around them to underscore the benefits of working with you as a partner. Show people what happens when they "go cheap." Sometimes you will lose to renegades; but if you do, make sure you follow up and document their performance to use as ammunition down the road. Performance risks are also related to your ability to reproduce and systematically deliver the differentiation value to your customers. Your superior performance has to be consistent and repeatable.

Industry recipes. This is similar to my thoughts earlier on changing a pricing metric. They also are mental blocks that industries suffer from. "People will never pay over $40 for a bag of cement" or "That is not the way we have always done it" is not only a powerful sentiment among change-resistant people within a company. It can also reflect how an entire market behaves. Habits can be hard to break, which is why I recommend that companies with a relatively small value pool work with establish metrics and selling approaches within the market, and that they focus on getting more from that system rather than changing the system itself.

Fairness. Fairness does not always mean "even." In this context, better synonyms are "reasonable" and "rational," which is another reason why you have to develop fact-based stories with a logic that customers can follow and appreciate. This is also why I insist that companies control their stories and communication in the market. Competitors will work to undermine your advantages, and professional buyers will use everything in their arsenals to neutralize them in order to wring price concessions and break a sales team's confidence. If you control the story, you can manage perceptions better, and fairness is all about perception.

Within these larger categories are a number of other moderators, both internal and external, that you may need to factor into your decision about how much of the value pool to capture. In my experience in pricing and marketing, these positive and negative moderators are often neglected or ignored. This might explain why leaders often default to a 50/50 split to share their value pool. Figure 7.5 is a long list of external moderators that can have a positive effect on how much of the value pool you can capture through pricing. I was able to identify eighteen of these positive external/market moderators through my experience in the VBP methodology and in the literature. The common denominator in many of these factors is skills and talent. Do you have a high-caliber sales team who can nurture strong customer relationships? Do you know your customers' processes inside and out? How strong is your storytelling, and how does it help you build your reputation?

External/market positive moderators:
- Intellectual property in the offering
- Degree of differentiation (inimitable)
- Degree of uniqueness of the offering
- Product/service performance consistency
- Strength and credibility of the value story
- Degree of product/service technical advantage
- Overall quality performance and consistency
- Ability to collect reliable customer value data
- Repeatability of differentiation value measurements
- Reputation as a price leader in the market
- Salesforce capabilities to extract price premium
- Technical intimacy with customer applications
- Credibility as an industry innovator
- Strength of brand equity and reputation
- Quality of customer relationship (intimacy)
- Price/quality relationship and perceptions
- Strategic innovation launch window
- Success value stories with early adopters

Figure 7.5. In isolation or combination, these moderators can all work in your favor.

The counterbalance to these positive factors is an equally extensive list of negative ones. Given that there are so many positive and negative mitigating or moderating factors, it amazes me even more that someone would reduce the dynamics of his or her market to the term "commodity" and conclude that the only thing that matters is price. Those situations are extremely rare. Figure 7.6 lists the negative external/market factors. The common denominator in many of these factors is behavior. How solid is your knowledge of how competitors may respond? What are the prevailing market attitudes toward discounts? Does the market have perceived price thresholds that you and competitors have been reluctant to cross? Sometimes these mental barriers are real and hard to penetrate. In other cases the risk was much less than anticipated. Often this involves crossing a "round" price point, such as $1 or $10.

External/market negative moderators:
- Fairness effect
- Overall industry competitive intensity
- Degree of industry commoditization
- Number of competitors in the market
- Risk of competitive pricing responses
- Competitive entrenchment at large customers
- Power of the unit of measure/industry recipes
- Product performance risk in application
- Power of distribution channels
- Customer discount expectations and mindset
- Psychology price ceiling and frames
- Power of large strategic customers
- High degree of customer concentration
- Pricing positioning perceptions
- Customer sensitivity analysis
- Price elasticity analysis
- Credibility of the value data and calculations
- Speed of technological obsolescence

Figure 7.6. These external moderators all work against you to some degree.

You may face internal challenges as well. Rare indeed would be a situation where a team agrees unanimously and without challenge to a recommendation on pricing. Almost everyone in an organization has an opinion on the organization's pricing practices, and most are not shy about sharing theirs. These internal moderators (see figure 7.7) can be positive or negative as well. The common denominators on the positive side are leadership and organizational readiness.

If an organization has a top-down commitment to value, a willingness to take risks, and open internal communication, it has a better chance of capturing more from the value pool than a company that is more risk averse, that is more siloed, and whose culture is characterized by fear rather than confidence. Pricing capabilities and maturity also make a difference. In my experience, the company that will still leave considerable money on the table, regardless of the size of its value pool, is one that features

Internal positive moderators:
- Strong commitment from top leadership
- Willingness to take calculated risks
- Potential incremental contribution margin
- Potential incremental impact of purchasing power
- Ability to do multifunctional teamwork
- Internal level of pricing maturity

Internal negative moderators:
- Internal market share mentality
- Level of internal misalignment (goals and comps)
- Lack of communication between teams
- Lack of internal confidence (commodity mindset)
- Focus on manufacturing/industrial goals
- Capacity absorption pressures
- Internal fear of failure
- Negative perception and experience with pricing

Figure 7.7. Your internal moderators represent both opportunities and challenges.

those negative factors plus a heavy "just make the sale" focus on market share or volume and that rewards its salespeople on volume, not on a mix of other measures. Narrow "commodity" thinking is a huge impediment.

These lists are long, so for simplicity's sake I suggest that you pick maybe a dozen moderators across all the lists, doing it in a balanced way. Human nature often leads us straight to the negative aspects, but I have found that internal confidence and trust are important assets. Yes, you should look at break-even and risk analyses, but you should still give the greatest weight to the value work you have done so far. You can't let the science slide and just hold your finger up to the wind now. Don't give in to fears or human nature and simply fold your cards now after making it this far. You spent all that time and did all that work, and confidence is essential when you take your new approaches and stories to customers in the field.

Without a high level of justifiable confidence, you risk a strong negative bias which manifests itself in the belief that you need lower prices to keep customers happy and win deals. If your value pool is large and positive, be assertive! Have the confidence to go and get it. Confidence starts internally and at the top of the organization. Don't talk yourself out of money when you have high differentiated value and a strong, rational story to support it.

You can use these fifty moderators in many ways. I developed a tool that allows users to pick a maximum of ten of them out of fifty, to give them an importance score on a scale of 1 to 10, and then a weight out of 100 points in the final value delivery. This process gives you a bit more robust approach to extracting a range of potential capture out of your value pool. It is not strictly scientific, but it balances intuition and rationality.

Organizations with a more negative bias are also prone to taking a narrow view about what generates value and what can contribute to the value pool. So I conclude this chapter with some examples of how companies can look beyond the product in order to find value, and how companies need to look at their value pool from two perspectives (reseller and end customer) when they sell their products through a multitier distribution system.

You can dollarize anything!

You do need to be fairly exhaustive in your dollarization approach to ensure that you extract all of your obvious and hidden differentiations and that you include them in your value pool. This means services and solutions as well as intangibles such as brand. Let's start with services. I am always excited when I hear stories about companies that have transitioned from being a product-focused company deriving over 80 percent of their revenue from unit sales to a service-oriented one deriving over 80 percent of their revenue from consulting and other services. And this happens all within the same industry with the same customers!

These companies accomplish this because they understand the value of all the things companies do, and they offer clients economically attractive alternatives. You can start down a similar path by following the steps shown in figure 7.8. Similar to what you would do in product development or in reverse-engineering, you are using a cross-functional team to understand how much it would cost you to deliver a particular service. Then you try to understand the cost that a customer incurs when they perform that service themselves. These services could be maintenance, application decisions, plant or supply chain management, or any other areas that a company could potentially outsource. If you can

- JIT deliveries
- EDI capabilities
- Supply-chain complexity management
- 24-hour job site in-person support
- Customized training programs
- Technical support by Skype
- 100% availability guarantee
- Specification support for complex tools
- Replacement warranties
- Marketing communications support

1 Assemble a multifunctional *team* of experts (finance, cost accounting, SCM, etc.).
2 Create a *spreadsheet*!
3 Start evaluating your *internal cost* for each service condition.
4 Identify *additional cost* for the customer if they had to do these services themselves.
5 Estimate the level of *goodwill* and premium of having these services available.
6 List all these *data points* in the spreadsheets.
7 Make a value estimation *decision*.
8 *Test* with friendly customers or partners.

Figure 7.8. Dollarizing the value of services.

document a way to offer that service more economically (cost savings) or do it better (creating a revenue opportunity), you have the ability to conduct a rational, value-based talk with customers.

Solutions and bundles present a more complicated challenge when you are trying to understand the value they provide and then dollarize it. The sticking point here is that many companies try to do this exercise holistically rather than break down the solution or the bundle into its constituent parts. The trick is to follow the path that you took when you looked at the value of an individual product; that is, you must understand your customers' needs and capabilities, and also your competitors' ability to provide solutions. With solutions and systems, as with services, you also need to consider "do it yourself" as a viable alternative.

You perform your value modeling on each individual component, then look at the value of overall solutions based on combinations of those components. Factors such as goodwill, brand, management quality, and reputation also matter at this stage. This process gives you the basis for defining a value pool for the solution and for making the same kinds of sharing decisions we discussed earlier in this chapter. The process is summarized in figure 7.9.

This is advanced modeling, and I could write an entire book on how to dollarize complex systems. You know customer dynamics and who the direct and indirect competitors for each component are, and you map the value for each component. This debundling, rebundling, and understanding of influencers each step of the way is the process you need to follow for very complex products such as airplanes, power plants, or other complex, multimillion dollar installations. An airplane isn't a product in the strict sense. It's a system.

Finally, we have the common situation where you sell through distribution. This could be sales through an industrial distributor or solutions provider, but the most challenging situation is

❶
**Understanding
the customer dynamics**

Buying center analysis
- Major influencers (I/E)
- Weight of procurement
- Technical experts' bid behavior

Needs analysis
- Technical needs
- Service needs
- Supply chain needs
- Risk profile

Customer value profile
- Technical
- Commercial
- Weighting
- Value/cost position

❷
**Understanding the
competition in the system**

Direct competition
- Component manufacturers
- System integrators
- Integration consultants

Indirect competition
- "Do nothing" or "as is"
- Internal customer process
- Internal consultants

❸
**Value modeling
of individual
components**

Component 1 vs.
competition:

Component 2 vs.
competition:

Project management:

Support and
maintenance

Other components:

❹
**Value modeling of
integrated system**

Systems with
components:

Systems without
components, includ-
ing goodwill, brand,
reputation, risk man-
agement factors:

❺
**Value-based price
setting and selling
strategy**

1   Set value-based
    prices.

2   Support sales'
    ability to sell on
    value.

3   Develop
    messaging.

Figure 7.9. Dollarizing the value of systems and solutions.

when you sell to consumers via a retailer. These B2B2C situations require two distinct value propositions and value stories, which means you have to expend twice the effort. You can't afford to skip one of these dollarization and story creation efforts if you want to know the full size of your value pool and take advantage of it. The retailer will require the kinds of argumentation you have created in this process so far: rational, fact-driven, professional, and fully dollarized, as I explain in figure 7.10.

The consumer story may also be dollarized, but it will depend heavily on an emotional component, too. You are using your stories to manage and influence perceptions. Getting close to consumers changes how you extract information, manage differentiation, and do the dollarization. Start by talking to customers first, getting their vocabulary, and getting the facts or a range of facts. But keep in mind that the benefits are often emotional in a way that may defy straightforward dollarization. As the advertising guru David Ogilvy once said, Coca-Cola doesn't go to market by saying it uses more cola berries than Pepsi does.

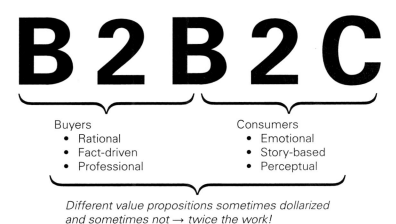

Figure 7.10. The challenge with B2B2C companies: Selling in a B2B2C environment requires two distinct value propositions.

Your strongest position comes when you can demonstrate a "pull" effect for the retailers, which means you can document that your value stories to consumers are driving demand in general—in the best case, demand at that particular retailer.

The same kinds of communication challenges exist in any multichannel situation, as described in figure 7.11. You have to understand who does what in your ecosystem, and therefore who is a recipient of messages and who is both a recipient and a multiplier. You need to understand who you are talking to and what kinds of value messages they want to hear on their own terms.

In this chapter you went from knowing your value pool to taking VBP decisions. You also looked at some more advanced applications of VBP. At this point you have completed all of your initial

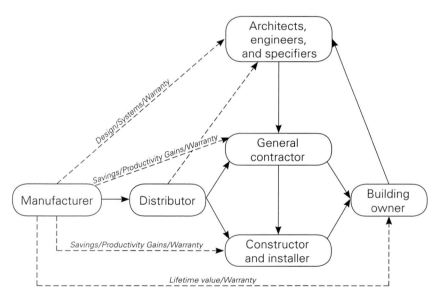

Figure 7.11. Stakeholders value map (dashed line = relational value messaging; solid line = transactional value messaging).Who needs what message, and who can serve as a multiplier?

homework; more importantly, you have progressed through the entire process in a way that is sensible, manageable, and repeatable.

You still need to implement what you have done, and you need to institutionalize it—not a trivial effort. You are about to undertake a change management effort, internally and externally, facing all the usual challenges in terms of resistance, communication, training, politics, and commitment. You are about to enter the world of the cynic, someone who, in the words of Oscar Wilde, "knows the price of everything, and the value of nothing." Success is by no means a given.

Some things to keep in mind

This chapter was quite rich in concepts and tips. Here are some additional key points for your dollarization process, your value pool calculation, and your price setting.

1 **Make sure you do not forget any critical elements of your differentiation.** The most critical ones need to be included in your value scorecard and in your value pool.

2 **Value pool calculations are going to be complicated to perform.** You might need to include lots of points. Remember to focus on a range or a ballpark number rather than on a precise number. We want to be relevant and credible. Do not tell the customer, "We have the potential to save $43,221.76 per year!" Tell the customer, "Working with us will save you anywhere between $40,000 and $50,000 per year. Let me tell you more."

3 **Internal value pool calculations have to stay internal.** They are for your eyes only. Not all customers will see or hear what's in the value pool or that it even exists. What goes out of your marketing machine might be completely different. This

A CYNIC IS SOMEONE WHO KNOWS THE PRICE OF EVERYTHING AND THE VALUE OF NOTHING.

—Oscar Wilde

gets back to the social and emotional intelligence needed for VBP. Credibility is more important than numbers and process.

4 **Relate your value pool to what you will be using it for.** If you use a customer value file or a value scorecard, relate the pool to the entire value of the portfolio and to the pricing of this portfolio. If you use it for a specific product pricing, you can be more specific in calculating the pool. That also requires agility and mindfulness.

5 Train your team well so that they do not mix up differentiators, moderators, value pool, and price setting. I see this happen a lot during training. Participants will include costs or their prices in the model. The value pool will be already impacted by external factors. To be able to compare apples to apples, it is important to find the *entire* value pool. Of course, it might be that no one pays the maximum price. But you have to find the value pool range in order to price well.

8

Managing Internal Resistance to Value-Based Pricing

Y OUR BIGGEST FIGHT WHEN *you embark*
on value-based pricing (VBP) may not be your
primary competitor or your nemesis across the table
when you negotiate with key accounts. It may be your
own organization. I don't shy away from insisting that
a VBP program be a declared, transparent priority. If
you are cooking this up in a secret back room, if people
are opting out of key meetings or postponing them, or
if what you are attempting is met with shoulder shrugs
or blank stares, then please stop! You are not ready to
pursue a full-scale VBP program. Doing so against those

headwinds means you are just burning through valuable resources.

In this chapter I describe the internal prerequisites for VBP, identify some warning signs that those prerequisites might not be fulfilled, and offer some ideas for how to scale things back so that you can pursue VBP with the appropriate odds for success.

Think you are ready to pursue value-based pricing? Try this quiz

You have to take this process seriously; paying lip service to it doesn't cut it. You need clear and affirmative answers to these questions *before* you get started. Implicit in these questions are the internal implementation barriers I see most often:

- Do you have a burning platform for customer value excellence?
- Is managing customer value one of your top strategic priorities?
- Is your top leadership's mindset aligned with value?
- Do you have the right collective confidence level?
- Do you have the right culture to embrace VBP?
- Do you have the right maturity and business orientation?
- Do you have too many strategic projects running at the same time?
- Is the timing right?

Let's look at some of these prerequisites in detail.

Burning platform for value. The platform may be there, but how close is it to the C-suite? The clamor for a value orientation could be buried in the organization. If it is too far away from the proper authorities, then this initiative won't go anywhere. You won't generate the awareness and garner the support, at least right now, for a large-scale project. You may complete steps 1 and 2 (know the competition; know the customer), and the organization will almost certainly see some benefits from that. Figure 8.1 shows many of the symptoms of a lack of value orientation.

You need the right context and the right agenda to start a value-based program. Who is asking for VBP? Who is driving the value agenda? Who is in charge of value right now? Why is it important to start right now? And what are our circumstances? Are we doing well? Sometimes there is a change of leadership and a move in general to value orientation. If VBP begins as a strategic initiative, it helps a lot with the implementation. If you begin with pricing, it's more complicated.

But if your business is in trouble, now is not the right time. Pursuing VBP during a crisis is not impossible, but it requires resources, attention, tools, and time. It may not be wise to divert resources from more pressing needs if the company's survival is

Lack of alignment around value:
- The C-suite wants value but still focuses on *volume* and market share.
- Value program activities are *disconnected* between functions and across divisions.
- There is no established *value dashboard* to track and communicate progress to the organization.
- *Discounting* behaviors do not change over time.
- Leaders claim value orientation in strategic statements but do not *execute* it in reality.
- *Execution* of traditional B2B marketing programs.
- Multiple *languages* in front of customers: R&D speaks innovation, marketing speaks value, and sales speaks discounts.
- *Short-term* volume-driven pricing actions occur at the end of the quarter or at end of the year.

Figure 8.1. These indicate that an organization lacks a value orientation.

under threat or if you are already dealing with tremendous market pressures. If you try to do VBP on a spare dime, people won't believe in it.

Top leadership mindset aligned with value. Are the leaders mindful? Do they see a need for more value creation, communication, and capture, or is it growth by volume and "let's open more plants"? Sometimes the head of the organization or division is an irrational denial person. In the face of tough competition in a low-growth market, they are in denial. They have a hope-for-the-best philosophy and bank on a market recovery. That is not a good philosophy.

Pricing solutions will not come on their own. Pricing is not a silver bullet that will solve internal competitive issues and structural problems. Pricers are not magicians. No one is going to hand you an envelope with the magic answer inside. You have to control your destiny; if you don't, someone else will.

It is a question of conviction from the top. Do they believe in the need for value, or is it smoke and mirrors? Are they serious about making tough changes? Are they willing to walk away from deals and to lose some level of market share? They understand that it is necessary, but it may still not change their long-held mindsets. You may also encounter passive-aggressive leaders who claim they want to do VBP but have another solution or agenda in mind. Typically, teams quickly discover this when the rubber meets the road and volumes start to go down for a while.

Even when top management commits to value, that step offers no guarantee that the existing organization can meet that goal. Confidence, culture, business maturity, focus, and a willingness to change are other prerequisites for a successful VBP journey. As you did in a couple of the previous chapters, listen closely to what you hear in the hallways and in meetings, and read between the lines in emails and other correspondence. The more frequently you hear change objections along the lines of what you see in figure 8.2, the greater the odds that your team falls short of meeting the prerequisites. These symptoms signal a deep-seated internal resistance to the kinds of mindset, behavioral, and procedural changes you will need to make.

Right collective confidence level. The logic behind confidence is clear. You can't project it if you don't have it. "Fake it until you make it" won't cut it with this program. If the team itself doesn't have faith in the new value-based approach, it will be impossible for them to explain and defend the new pricing strategy and price points when they meet customers. You have to have some courage. You have to have a collective belief that you can do the hard work and make the tough decisions if needed. The pricing team needs to believe that the salesforce can be good at value selling and value communication. And the salesforce needs to believe that the pricing team has the proper VBP skills. And then everyone needs to have confidence in the business model and the level of differentiation. This is the challenge!

Standard internal change objections:
- It will never work in our business unit.
- We are selling commodities and have no differentiation.
- Our customers just do not care about value.
- We have always done it this way, and it works.
- Our issues are temporary, and pricing will get better.
- The market sets the prices for our products and services.
- Now is not the right time to launch a value project.
- OK, here is another "project du jour."
- We have too many projects right now. Too busy for that.
- Let us wait for the end of the quarter and see what happens.

Figure 8.2. Common statements or coping mechanisms that reflect organizational resistance.

It is difficult to make bold moves in pricing models, so it is no surprise that confidence might need some reinforcement. To complete the dollarization process, you need confidence in your data. You will need to invest in the quality of your competitive and customer data, so that you can build a base of confidence that will help you with decisions later on. "Garbage in, garbage out" will undermine your confidence in your value pool and the price points you have set using it as a guide.

To complete the VBP journey successfully, you also need confidence in each other. Have you had some pricing debacles in the past? If so, how well did you overcome them? These past successes and failures will greatly affect your ability to move forward with decisions. I talk more about this below when we look at maturity of the organization.

Right culture. The right culture to embrace VBP is characterized by collaboration, alignment, and accountability. If you have differences in goals, disconnects between functions, and no central tracking or communication, it will be hard for you to align around value. You may go through the motions and do more "value stuff," but behaviors won't improve unless and until the ingrained practices in an individual department also change. If that doesn't happen, there is no collective alignment around what to do and why. You have multiple languages and vocabulary in front of the customer, so they are confused. You have raised expectations, but if the culture prevents you from embracing value, it will be very difficult to implement VBP.

Right maturity level and business orientation. One of the most important tests of your organization's maturity level and business orientation is how you use the word "commodity." If this is a common way for you to describe your products—internally and especially externally—you shouldn't be surprised if customers treat you as a commodity, meaning they argue that you have no differentiation. They have no desire at all to pay a premium. A commodity mindset shows that you don't have the right business orientation for VBP.

Given maturity and a business orientation, there is also a difference between going through the motions and making the required changes and improvements. The volume-versus-value mindset is decisive. It is often the acid test for a transformation and for whether an organization is serious about it. Think back to the end of your previous fiscal quarter: if you were still thinking in terms of volume and making decisions based on volume goals, you are

wasting your time if you try to dive into VBP. You can spend all the money you want and create the culture you want, but if your organization is not willing to let go of market share, it will not change. Pretty brutal, but true.

The market share mindset is the antithesis of a value mindset. It is the Jack Welch "be number 1 or number 2" mentality that still determines the way so many Gen Xers and Gen Yers run their businesses. I find it almost surreal in some companies that make market share into one of their most important and most reported KPIs.

One key aspect of organizational maturity is whether the pricing and marketing functions exist already. A big warning sign is that you have neither on your org chart.

What role has the pricing team played historically? In some companies, the pricing organization is visible and has a strong advisory role, if not a decision-making one. In other organizations (primarily cost-focused ones), pricing has more of a clerical function. If the latter type of organization switches to a VBP focus, let's be honest: no one will inherently believe it. That is another reason why you need to begin the transition by establishing a thorough understanding of differentiated value and then make pricing decisions. Do not try to do pricing on the fly, before you have looked at value properly.

What role has the marketing team played historically? You need to have some kind of marketing base to get started. Without a strong inclination toward research and the right levels of customer intimacy, it will be difficult to do so. Maturity is about taking a more progressive approach to communication. If you are still sending out brochures and building your marketing efforts around trade fairs, you are using 20th-century techniques. Maturity is also about data: collecting it, connecting it, and using systems and IT. If you are still using manual approaches to track data and do analyses, you aren't leveraging and mining the data to its full extent.

Making value and value-based pricing a priority

Even if you have the right cultural basis, the right mindset, and the right organizational strengths, there is still something that can doom a VBP initiative: internal competition. If you have too many priorities and competing initiatives, it will be difficult for you to make VBP a success. I realize that enthusiasm for projects can come in waves even in reasonably disciplined companies. It is possible that VBP bubbles up to the top of a long list of great ideas. You need to make a choice in those situations, and keep the medium- and long-term consequences in mind.

In other words, if something is important, then it's important. And that means someone will have to do the work. They will need VBP-related tasks built into their objectives and in some cases their job descriptions. Some companies have so many people on so many projects that all they seem to do is move from meeting to meeting. That is a clear sign that the company has taken on too much.

You can't make a sudden commitment to VBP. You can't wake up one morning and declare *"aha, we are ready!"* This is *not* a training program where you teach people how to fill out EVE sheets. VBP requires lots of practice, many iterations, lots of repetition, and lots of communication. If it is project 15 on the company's to-do list, it will be difficult to get time, attention, and other resources. If it is the project du jour, you may get a burst of resources and support, but these won't be sufficient or sustainable. So ask yourself honestly: How many initiatives do you have? Can you integrate VBP into what you already have? Is there a customer intimacy program or a marketing transformation that you can fold it into? You may find a way to fold other priorities together into the VBP initiative.

If you have these symptoms, what is the cure?

If the stars align across all the prerequisites I've mentioned above, congratulations! You can afford to move at a faster pace and set a more aggressive timeline for your VBP initiative. But if you meet real, deep-seated resistance, you will have to modify your expectations and your approach. You can't force the issue, as I show in the comic in figure 8.3. So what do you do?

While I still believe that VBP is an all-or-nothing program because of its depth and its duration, you don't have to abandon the idea of value-based work entirely. Real life dictates that you move at your own pace in your current environment, and at an

Figure 8.3. Better to infiltrate than dominate.

intensity you can handle while still getting things done. Instead of attacking the entrenched mindsets of the volume, market share, and cost-and-competition fortresses head-on, with all your might, you will have to be more subtle.

You will have to infiltrate.

You can find your pace even when you don't have a pace, by choosing some of these smaller-scale initiatives.

User-need segmentation. Most companies periodically review and renew their segmentations. Find out when such an exercise is in the offing, and use it as an opportunity to establish some value-based thinking. Get yourself a seat at the table and work to introduce needs-based criteria, without trying to throw all of the existing criteria overboard. This can pave the way for participation and influence in the regular discussions around price changes.

Price changes. This an excellent opportunity to plug some basic VBP tools into the price management process. You can introduce the concept of value maps and get the teams comfortable with populating them and using them as guidance. You can also weave in some value modeling, even if you don't show the full-fledged EVE tool right away (most likely a wise move!). You can also start talking up the idea that price changes should reflect differentiated value rather than cost and competition, while avoiding wholesale changes or denigrating the existing approaches.

New product development. This is probably your most powerful entry point if you want to follow the "infiltration" route to VBP. A new product development process is ostensibly about value, often involves direct consumer research and testing, and often is done in a spirit of openness and experimentation. You will need some intensive training to bring your innovation teams up to speed on the ideas of differentiated value, including perceived value and willingness-to-pay. If the teams get a feel for the power of the concepts, and adopt some of the new vocabulary, you will have achieved a small but important victory. Each organization has its own language, but establishing a working vocabulary around value terminology helps establish a common basis for all departments (new product development, marketing, sales, finance).

Service innovation. This is a possibility in a manufacturing company as well, not just in a service-focused one. Similar to new product development, you should have many opportunities here to make value an additional criterion when the company makes a go/no-go decision on a new service. Help the development team get comfortable with the tools and vocabulary of VBP.

Versioning of offerings. One size does not fit all. As companies get better at recognizing customer needs, they need specific product variants to match those needs. This is an ideal opportunity for the company to price those products based on perceived, differentiated value and not (solely) on cost differentials or competitive position. Because these are additional to the portfolio rather than core products, the company might be more likely to embrace a new approach and get some proof that VBP can help the company meet its financial and commercial goals more easily.

Some things to keep in mind

1 **Your organization needs to do the VBP work itself.**
    This means you need to customize the approach to your dynamics and your maturity level. The VBP process is an

umbrella, but you don't have to go to 100 percent when you design your program. Design it to match your circumstances.

2 **Go incrementally and infiltrate rather than generate confusion and rejection.** Do it for a small number of products by taking a mindful approach about what is needed. You need to create success stories and bring others on board, in line with a traditional change management process. To get started, you may need to pare down the program and the expectations, then add sophistication later. Don't go all out and storm the fortress if the soldiers inside are not prepared to accept what you have to offer.

3 **VBP, done properly, involves lots of changes and lots of hard work.** That is one of the main reasons why only a fraction of companies really do VBP to its full extent and reap the full value from it. Most companies underestimate the scope of the VBP agenda and succumb to simplified case studies they hear at conferences or from consultants. Change management is key, and maximizing the chances of execution success depends on the quality of the project design.

4 **Keep in mind that process excellence is not the end goal of VBP.** I often see companies focusing too much on tools, processes, and standard methods. The issue is not just getting the process right. The issue is getting people to jump on board and getting them to use simple and agile tools.

5 **VBP requires resources and people doing the work.** Someone will have to lead the charge, organize the meetings, create the value tools, collect the data, and so forth. Who is that someone?

Do something rather than nothing. Infiltrate if necessary.

9

Managing External Barriers to Value-Based Pricing

THE EXTERNAL HEADWINDS BLOW *from many directions when you try to implement value-based pricing (VBP) and bring your trade partners on board. Customers can object to your line of argument and your differentiation claims, so you need to prepare for these challenges. The ones with professional buyers will know what you have been up to, step by step, and will have their ammunition ready. Then there are market realities you cannot ignore. How do you do VBP when your market is commoditizing? How do you deploy VBP when your competitors are habitual price-cutters? How do you manage the complexity of VBP on a global scale?*

Managing value with your channel partners

Let's start with trade partners. Even if you do not have trade channels in your value chain, you should read this section. Your analyses enabled you to quantify a value pool, write compelling segment-specific value propositions, and set prices, all with end customers in mind. They are the ones who ultimately benefit from the value your products and services generate. Between you and them are usually trade partners, often layers of them, who have their own interests and who want to tap into the value pool you have created.

You have to get these trade partners on board the value train! If you are using distributors of any sort, even retailers, it will be a challenge to reach end customers and extract the right amount of value on your own. It is imperative that you help your distributors also sell value, even if it means an extensive training program accompanied by new incentives. They have to understand what you are doing and facilitate rather than hinder it. They also have to be incentivized to support your value programs. Otherwise, they will lump you in with the other undifferentiated products on the shelf, effectively silencing your value messages. Figure 9.1

Best practices to bring channels on board the value journey:
- Create *differentiated programs* exclusively for trade partners.
- Create *value models* for trade channels to help sell value better.
- Engage with top leaders and *owners*.
- Design dedicated *training programs* (value selling, differentiation, dollarization, product performance, technical support).
- Design specific *incentives* program for channel staff.
- Increase focus on *end users* to boost demand and establish market pricing (MSRP).
- Design *loyalty* clubs and programs.
- Offer *point-of-sale communication* and branding support.

Figure 9.1. Best practices for getting trade partners excited and engaged about value.

shows some of the best practices you can adopt in your efforts to help your trade partners undertake their own value journey on the same roads as you. The list is not exhaustive, but it is a good start for you to think about concrete programs.

The dealers can be a dramatic value bottleneck if you don't bring them on board *during* the VBP process instead of after it. Some of them will be sensitive to more changes and disruption because of losses they may have incurred when the market shifted more toward e-commerce platforms. You need to show some understanding if not empathy for the challenges that some of your channel partners may have faced. It is harder for you to make a positive argument for change when disruption has mostly been their enemy, not their friend, over the last couple of decades as terms such as disintermediation, omnichannel, and e-commerce turned out to be much more than fancy-sounding fads. These have made some of them more protective of their margins than ever and less receptive to yet another potentially disruptive change.

Against this backdrop, how do you convert your distribution into value partners who multiply and transmit value rather than impede it? And how do you accomplish this when they have different goals, different pricing processes, and different behaviors? There are steps you can take, which is why I labeled figure 9.1 "best practices." I would like to highlight and elaborate on some of them.

Create differentiated programs. Your channel partners probably serve different customer segments, and there is a good chance that these segments will have some alignment with the way you have segmented the same customers according to needs and value. This alignment creates opportunities for you to tailor programs that support what the distributors do in the market and what value they add in their segment. In the same way that there is no one-size-fits-all approach to customers, you will create unnecessary tension and conflict if you pursue such an approach to your channels. This variety can also be reflected in the incentives you provide the staff at your channel partners. Some distributors are pure order-takers, while others have trained specialists who contribute more to the value chain. Your incentives should reflect and reward this.

Engage with the top leaders and owners. The shift for some of your channel partners may be too significant, or the incentives too large, for you to make this a bottom-up exercise. Think of your channel partners the same way you did your own organization: value commitment starts at the top and flows to the bottom, not the other way around. Top leaders and owners should be able to grasp the concept of strategic fit, business differentiation, and long-term value programs.

Design dedicated training programs. Similarly, you cannot expect your channel partners to go from 0 to 60 mph in two seconds, as if they were the Lamborghinis of value. Value selling, differentiation, and dollarization may be entirely new concepts for them, in the sense that you use these terms. Some of your channel partners may be familiar with your product performance and technical support—they may even provide some of the latter—but VBP has changed the perspective and drawn more attention to them. So it also means giving your dealers' sales and marketing teams simple and compelling value tools designed for their needs and their staff: value scripts, segmentation guides, value propositions, point-of-sale value messages, and so forth.

Increase focus on end users. Value selling is not something you can delegate to your channel partners. In a true partnership, which you should incentivize and reward, you will also do your part to boost demand and communicate your desired prices (MSRP or list) with confidence. In markets without list prices, your task is to emphasize the value and benefits of your products and services, and also to show how certain channel partners, or types of channel partners, can support that value proposition. You can't take your eyes off your end users as you bring your channel partners on board. They are two parts of the same value ecosystem.

To say that the distributors are "stuck" between suppliers and buyers is to be too focused on the negative. Your own starting viewpoint should be to look at how they already add value and how well what they do matches up with your new view of the value chain. You need to understand your ecosystem and what your value chain looks like, but most importantly, you need to control the value story across all steps of your ecosystem. In some ways your partners are already part of the story. Build on the positives first instead of treating them as a barrier between you and your end users rather than as a channel to them.

Building on the positive also applies to how you approach your current customers, regardless of whether you sell directly or through channels. You need to start with your value partners, the ones on the far right of figure 9.2. You need to identify the pioneers among your customers, or at least those who will get the value story right away. They will become the opinion leaders in the industry, and they can help you document the value data and turn assumptions into facts you can use to augment your value story. Trying to introduce everything to everybody at the same time makes no sense.

The verification and validation you earn by working with your value partners will make your story much more robust and your

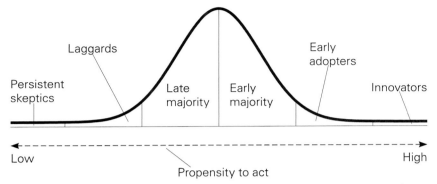

Figure 9.2. Start with your value partners...show success, document wins, and win the heart of the early majority. Look to the far right when you begin rolling out the value-based-pricing results to your customers.

value models much stronger when you need to convince the late majority and the laggards to accept your new messages and your new prices. Consider yourself to be in a testing mode. You need cooperation from customers, and the value partners (innovators, early adopters) are your best candidates. When you work with the early adopters, you can establish the anchors for value in your industry. Their actions and their responses set the perception of value in the market. That makes it easier to engage others later on in your value-based process.

Managing value in your ecosystem

You may have gotten the impression during your VBP process that there is an important world for you to tap beyond your narrow value chain. I call this the value ecosystem and show some of its participants in figure 9.3.

Your narrow value chain includes an obvious subset of these parties, such as manufacturers, suppliers, distributors, and competitors. But everyone on that list is a potential partner in your efforts to create, defend, sustain, and above all communicate

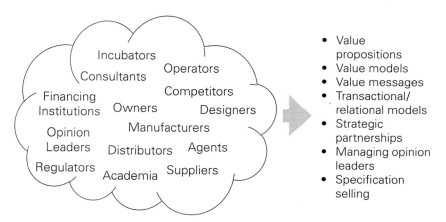

Figure 9.3. Managing your ecosystem for value. The world of value extends far beyond your narrow value chain.

value. Your VBP was not undertaken to benefit you only today, with your current portfolio. It should become even more important in the future, as you renovate and innovate. This is a much more attractive spirit and proposition for designers, incubators, and financial institutions, who are by definition eager to create value and profit from it. Consultants and academics are always on the lookout for new case studies, success stories, best practices, and new processes. While the intimate details of business by nature need to remain secret, the fact that you are successful should not be secret. Look throughout the ecosystem for potential partners who have an interest not only in spreading your gospel but in learning from it as well. One critical comment here is that you will have to signal to the ecosystem that your value journey is serious and for the long term. This is even more relevant when you are the first company in the ecosystem making the bold move to gain value leadership. Going first is a difficult step. It requires an intentional and purposeful communication campaign around value in the ecosystem.

Managing objections: Preparation is crucial to beating the buyers

"Beating the buyers" may sound aggressive, but you have to appreciate their role in their organizations and their training to perform it. They want you to believe that you operate in a world full of easy alternatives and commodities. Unless you have clear, high, unequivocal value—essentially an unbeatable value proposition—it is their job to make you believe you are fully replaceable, your value claims are exaggerated sales talk, your perception of value is distorted, and your prices have air in them. Even trusted value partners will offer some resistance or at least require you to provide some value defense. No one gets a blank check. So they are certainly geared up to win, to beat you.

You will meet with tons of objections. Your sales and marketing teams will have to prepare for these objections and become excellent at responding with critical value messages. In essence, we have to regain the upper hand in the "message war" and slowly modify the perceptions of buyers. Buyers may demand that you justify your differentiation and prove rationally that you have it. They won't take what you say at face value unless you prove it. Lots of objections means you have lots of opportunities for failure. This can be overwhelming at first, because it is literally impossible for you to be prepared for every objection a buyer may raise. At the same time, you won't succeed if every response to their objections is improvised. To give you a starting point to prepare to counter the most common objections, I have grouped them into the three categories shown in figure 9.4.

You have to have credible documentation of your performance differential, and not just one or two anecdotes. You need an army and an arsenal of documentation, and you may need to deploy those communication assets on multiple fronts. Documentation

❶ Disagreement about what matters
- Issues with definitions, terms, and approaches
- Disagreement about scope of the value models and scorecards
- Inability to influence other parties to share information and collaborate
- Goal conflict between the two organizations

❷ Inability to quantify value
- Lack of access to buying center outside of procurement
- No trust and cooperation from customers to validate value data
- Unwillingness to collaborate on value initiatives
- Lack of know-how with customer on how to calculate and capture value

❸ Difficulty in sharing value pool
- Buyers who understand value approach but ask for more value for them
- Issues with industry recipes, mental locks, and value bottlenecks
- Weak negotiation position when facing powerful buyers
- Lack of trust in value delivery ("value at risk")

Figure 9.4. Dealing with objections to your value proposition starts with understanding and prioritizing them.

is your ammunition against all the potential fronts of failure, rejection, and resistance.

The first front of potential failure is interpretation. You and the buyer may disagree on what matters. Economic Value Estimation (EVE) almost by definition is open to interpretation. What precisely do the drivers mean? What units are you using to measure value? Customers may have different interpretations because of their goals, because they have no internal benchmarks for value, or because they themselves cannot "sell" your message internally. All of these are legitimate concerns, and the burden of proof—at least when you begin implementing VBP—is always on you, not them. When you enter into a value conversation, who is across the table? How open are they to technical assessments and collaboration, which may include access to plants?

The second opportunity for failure is the inability to quantify value. One primary reason for this is the customer's unwillingness to collaborate on a value initiative. This leaves you in a catch-22. You can't meet their burden of proof without access to their processes, data, and plants, but they deny you access and then penalize you for not proving your value. Part of this may be a standoffish attitude, and part of it may be that they themselves lack the internal talent or expertise to measure value in the way you need it for your EVE.

The third area of potential failure is the sharing of the value pool. Some customers will say "all for me." Some may challenge that you will not or even cannot deliver the value you have promised. They may have come to this conclusion on their own, or they may have heard this message from a competitor. They may also put so much faith in industry rules of thumb and mental algorithms that any departure from them is uncomfortable and thus undesirable. So they seek a greater share of the value pool as a form of insurance or risk mitigation. A small company micromanaged by the owner can be especially difficult in this regard.

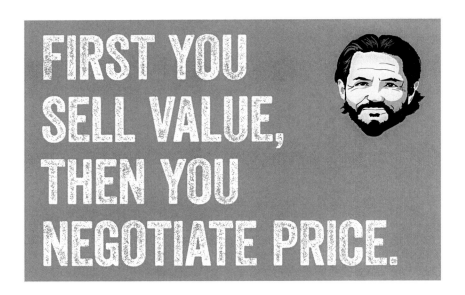

This is all the more reason why it is essential that you demonstrate and convince them of the value, and then work with them to track it. This is also where soft skills come into play. Numbers don't win battles on their own. You need to help your numbers make their case. Understand who is on the other side of the table, what their motivations are, and what they are measured against. First you sell value, then you negotiate price.

Managing and meeting objections is something within your control, and preparation is key. But what about the things beyond your direct control? Remember, competitors are part of your value ecosystem and what they do—or don't do—changes the context you operate in.

Managing responses from competition

What happens if you are the only one who does VBP? Once again, VBP is not about achieving the highest price but rather the right price based on the relative value you provide. If your competition is erratic, you may need to make some moves as well. But you have to make intelligent moves, not tit-for-tat countermeasures or overreactions. Fall back on the guidance you developed and vetted in your preparation phases. You need to use value maps and make your value modeling process very dynamic. When faced with erratic competitors and price cutters, you will have to adapt quickly and adopt an agile approach. Get creative on the product and service side, because you have quantified the value of the components of what you sell, not just the complete product or solution. You may need to bundle, use second brands, or offer some services for free to offset the competition's offering without threatening your core sources of value. The point is that you need to track the competition. You can't stay static. You need to stay relevant.

I have seen cases where a company could justify a 25 percent premium, but if someone undercuts them, there is only so much they can do. The two basic options are to raise value or cut price. If someone has made a move to disturb your position, you may have to reduce your price. VBP is not a spell you can use to hypnotize your customers into paying higher prices, nor is it a cleaning agent that dissolves and dissipates all your consistently overly aggressive competitors. On the other hand, the preparation you have done so far has given you a solid foundation. You can now be flexible with confidence, as you switch value drivers, try other approaches, or look for ways to counter what your competitors have done. By now in this book, you are supposed to know your competitors as well as they know themselves. Did you rise to that challenge? If you have, you should know whether their latest price move was tactical or strategic. You have to know your price cutters. If pricing in your market is super dynamic, you need the right maps and models, and you need to constantly monitor changes. That is simply the reality of business. If you go in with a premium you can't defend, then you haven't done your homework.

Managing value in a commoditizing market

This is an internal objection I hear often from teams I work with. How can we do VBP when the entire market is spiraling in price wars and commoditization? That is an excellent question! I often remind them that lots of companies disappear every year because of acquisition, price wars, or bankruptcy. My standard answer is "What choice do you have? How long can you reduce your price without going out of business?" Price cuts are quantitative. The qualitative side of that coin is the perception that your market is commoditizing. If that is the case, you can't give up. You have to be creative and start fighting back. You have to invest in innovation to start changing the conversation from price to value. Use bundling, versioning, or other tactics to find or create pockets of differentiation. One opportunity that may be harder to capitalize on is to begin charging for some services that have been free, either historically or as a response to the economic crisis of 2008–9. At that time, many companies gave away services as a way to maintain volume. When markets recover and companies look to improve or re-establish their pricing power, services such as JIT delivery or technical training are candidates for prices, because they create measurable value. Debundling is also a possibility, as airlines have done with so many services. But you still need to keep the context in mind. You can add surcharges, and you can differentiate performance levels, but it may be difficult to reintroduce a fee on something that has been free for many years.

Managing value-based pricing globally

Finally, you may have heard the term "glocal," a combination of global strategies and local tactics. That is a very good description of what you face if you deploy VBP on a global scale. The perception of value and the acceptance of premiums is subject to tradition and can be different in each culture. That means that while your basic EVE structure may be similar around the world, you need local versions and local value models. Perceptions and traditions—some deeply held—mean you need to act differently in, say, Europe, Brazil, or Indonesia. Even within these vast, populous countries or regions, you may need further value breakdowns. That adds to the complexity of managing value at the global level. It requires a much more holistic approach to pricing strategy and a lot more cross-functional and cross-cultural collaboration.

Some things to keep in mind

1 **You will face lots of internal and external barriers when deploying VBP.** Good preparation matters for both. Going into the design process, you need to plan for resistance and potential failure. The sooner, the better!

2 **Launching a value approach in an industry is not for everyone.** It requires market and industry leadership in the value chains and the overall ecosystem. It also means having the courage and conviction to take a different route than competitors. This is not just a pricing discussion. It includes innovation and marketing as well.

3 **Succeeding at VBP requires lots of change management work.** That includes building a winning coalition both internally and externally. Traditionally, change efforts focus on internal change. But you cannot succeed without your key partners in the market. Value is not a unilateral effort. It is about building a value coalition to move an entire industry mindset.

4 **Commoditization is just another word for lack of imagination.** You will hear about commoditization at every step of your VBP deployment. Avoid that trap. Keep fighting it and turn this negative energy into positive actions for innovation.

10

Operationalizing Value-Based Pricing as Part of Value-Based Strategies

ONE REASON WHY EVERYONE *in an organization has an opinion about pricing is that questions about pricing and especially about value come up in almost everyone's day-to-day activities. Value emanates from your organization whether you like it or not. The challenge lies in controlling those impressions— how the company consciously creates, measures, communicates, extracts, and monitors value—rather than leaving value to chance or luck. There is a discipline to value communication.*

Based on the work you have completed so far, you are well positioned to take conscious control of value in other activities, not merely pricing. It starts with value-based innovation, and continues with value-based marketing and value-based selling. Ultimately you will create a culture of value in your organization, manifested in the organization's whole mindset. Value becomes second nature, and you must remain vigilant to keep it that way.

Sometimes it may seem as if completing and maintaining all of your necessary EVE sheets is the heart-and-soul of value-based pricing (VBP). Those sheets are indeed a fundamental part of VBP, but let's not get completely lost in the rows and columns of your Excel sheets. VBP is far more than just doing EVEs! It is the basis for your go-to-market strategy, and it touches on the pillars of marketing strategy: segmentation, differentiation, communication. I recommend that you think in terms of value-based strategies and not restrict your activities to VBP.

The first place you implement a value-based strategy is pricing, because the new, dollarized value propositions hone your communication skills and demand rigor and discipline. They are also likely to improve your financial situation, generating higher profits that you can invest in other areas. Pricing is where the stimulus comes from. It demands so much strategic alignment from strategy that you have to look at your strategy as a whole.

Figure 10.1 shows the spectrum of areas where a dollarized value proposition can also play a critical role. Value is a discipline across the whole organization, and you need a high level of internal discipline and execution to ensure that value becomes

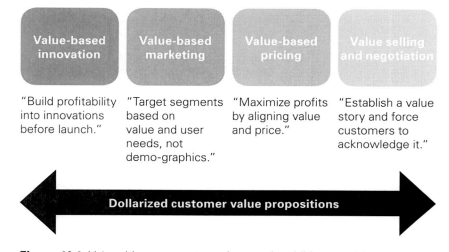

"Build profitability into innovations before launch."   "Target segments based on value and user needs, not demo-graphics."   "Maximize profits by aligning value and price."   "Establish a value story and force customers to acknowledge it."

Figure 10.1. Value drives many strategic areas in addition to pricing.

embedded in everything you do. It starts with value-based innovation.

Value-based innovation: Learn to set the value bar high

You should gear your innovation and new product development toward creating a unique value proposition and differentiation. Peter Thiel makes this a core premise of his book *Zero to One* and writes that "indeed the single most powerful pattern I have noticed is that successful people find value in unexpected places, and they do this by thinking about business from first principles instead of formulas." In other words, they ask themselves the basic questions that I mentioned in chapter 5, the questions that are central to your business and for which you need shared answers: Who are and *aren't* our customers? Why are we different? How do we add value?

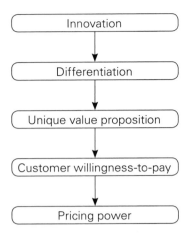

Figure 10.2. The route from value-based innovation to value-based pricing.

These are the questions or the points that drive value-based innovation, as I show in figure 10.2. Historically, most innovation processes such as Stage-Gate focus on cost or competition. How can we deliver a product at a lower cost or take cost out of a process? How can we outdo the competition in areas X and Y? These are two of the reasons why so many innovations do not fulfill their profit potential. Their creators failed to identify the customers' problems up front. What are their hidden needs, their customer pains or gains? What unexpected places hide untapped pockets of value? These are the questions that ultimately lead to differentiation and allow you to craft a unique value proposition, something no one else has and that no one else can quickly replicate. Can you insist on setting the bar that high in your organization and keeping it there?

There has to be a match between the value you create and communicate and your ability to extract value. Customers must demonstrate some willingness-to-pay. The higher this is, and the more differentiated your value proposition is, the greater your pricing power. Companies stray from this path in the R&D processes when they focus primarily or exclusively on just two Cs— cost and competition—instead of including the customer C in the mix and basing prices on value. I address the consequences of this in the comic in figure 10.3. In essence, we need a shift in how R&D projects hit the market. Instead of pricing developed mostly on costs, you should have innovation projects that are based on customer needs whose pricing is developed based on willingness-to-pay. The sooner you begin this switch in innovation focus, the easier the back end of the value approach gets.

To ensure that you don't end up spinning the wheel right before you launch your product, you have to start quantifying value early on in your Stage-Gate process. Value has to be central to your discussions, to facilitate the formal delivery and sharing of value information throughout the process. If these ideas are foreign to

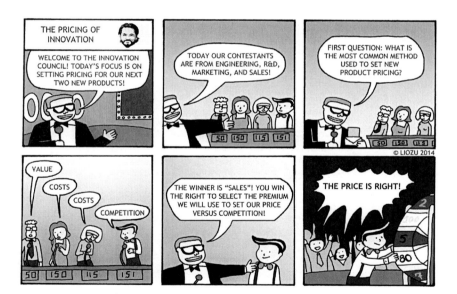

Figure 10.3. Do you want to base your prices on value...or chance?

the new product development team, you can offer to do an EVE early on. Use the innovation process as a way to infiltrate, introducing segmentation as well and not just the concepts and tools of EVE. You will know you have reached an important milestone, one that matters for your team, your customers, and your bottom line, when you succeed in making value, instead of cost and competition, the basis for go/no-go decisions. What impact do these changes have? You do better innovation and better value management and introduce better products at a higher price.

I have already mentioned some of the tools for uncovering hidden customer needs, customer pains to be solved, and customer gains to be created. Figure 10.4 offers a longer list. The threads common to these ten items are listening, observing, and digging. Often, great value-based innovations require progressive voice-of-customer programs. They demand a great level of customer intimacy. Superficial views lead to superficial conclusions. You need a deep understanding of what customers do—and *could* do—from different perspectives in order to have a good chance of discovering a valuable need you can meet better and sooner than anyone else.

Innovation tools to discover customer hidden needs:
- Leading user meetings, panels, and councils
- Customer advisory boards
- Community of enthusiasts and brand evangelists
- Market and technology radars
- Signal analysis from near and far industries
- Customer process mapping and blueprinting
- A *day in the life of a customer* brainstorming
- Customer observations and ethnographic research
- Workflow studies
- Industry patent search and analysis

Figure 10.4. You have many ways to identify your customers' valuable hidden needs.

I'd like to highlight patent search and analysis at this point. While they do not automatically imply that there is willingness-to-pay and enough value to extract, patents are an indirect indicator of an industry's inventiveness, its ability to find solutions no one else has come up with or to make meaningful improvements to existing solutions. Have we become more or less inventive over the last 30 years? The United States granted around 72,000 utility patents and 5,000 design patents in 1985. Over the span of 30 years, those numbers exploded to 300,000 and 26,000, respectively. American companies are clearly creating more unique products and designs. Have we seen a comparable explosion in value? Are they creating four times the *value* today that they did in the mid-1980s? That is the key question, and looking at widely reported statistics about new product failures, I would say the answer is no. That is all the more reason for *value analysis* from the outset of new product development processes. You'll see this concept illustrated in figure 10.5.

Start with value, finish with price

You start with value and finish with price. I suggest measuring expected *differential* economic value (EDEV). The reason and the logic should be obvious by now: why would you invest in making something that doesn't create a significantly sized value pool, or that doesn't add to an existing one? You have to do your value homework, to avoid misreading the value or not catching that competitors could quickly neutralize your newly created value.

The Stage-Gate process in figure 10.5 focuses on value at every stage and specific deliverables at each gate. This is an especially important addition in engineering-driven companies, where teams tend to think there is an intrinsic customer appeal in better or more sophisticated technology. In the words of the famous

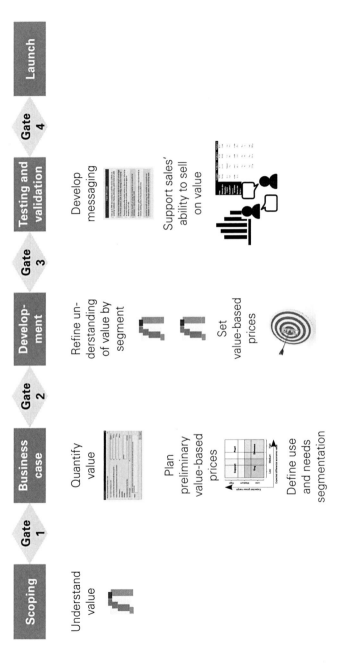

Figure 10.5. Embed value understanding and quantification at each step of the Stage-Gate process.

architect Louis Sullivan, "form follows function." To paraphrase that in your context, value (and thus the form of the product or service) follows a clear customer need. You still have to take costs into account, of course, because some very valuable customer features and benefits may be too costly for you to deliver reliably, at least right now. But incorporating value—or, more specifically, segment-specific EDEV—into each step of the process ensures that customers will want the product you are developing, and will pay for it.

You see the role that costs play in figure 10.6, a matrix that allows you to group the products in your pipeline according to their chances of being a financial and commercial success. The dream is to come up with pearls, the products that generate high value for the customer and high margins for you. These are unfortunately

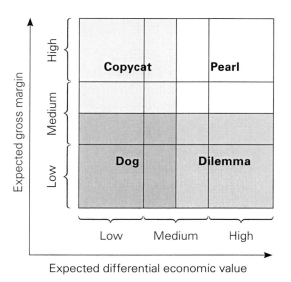

Figure 10.6. Screening innovation projects: Seeking pearls, solving dilemmas, and avoiding dogs.

the rarest kind. Your engineering and process talent may allow you to develop high-margin products, but if the EDEV is low, you have basically created a copycat product, although one that may earn you some money if you can succeed in stealing share from incumbents.

The challenging ones, which I have labeled dilemmas, offer high EDEV but do not promise higher margins for your company. You face a tough question: Launch the product anyway because of its strong customer appeal, then figure out over time how to lower costs without sacrificing benefits? Or do you kill the project—despite its high EDEV—because you can't afford to make it? Maybe there is an intelligent trade-off, in which you sacrifice some of the customer value in order to improve margins, thereby moving the product closer to a pearl or to a copycat. You may have one compelling feature that is driving up costs dramatically. What if you reconfigure the product without that feature? These important discussions can make or break a great idea. You can only have these discussions in a rational way and make sound decisions when you make customer value one of your essential evaluation criteria.

The period right after you launch the product is a sensitive time. Your focus on customer value continues. As I mentioned before, you should focus your initial sales and marketing efforts on your best customers and partners. They are the early adopters who can understand your value, validate it, and accept the initial prices you have set. Success in this phase is primarily a communications challenge. You will have to work collaboratively within your organization across many functions (innovation, product development, pricing, technology, sales) to develop value and pricing programs, and at the same time work diligently with customers to educate them and earn their buy-in to your value propositions. I summarize these recommendations in figure 10.7.

Value and pricing in early stage of product life cycle:
1 Focus heavily on mapping *value proposition* for the business model.
2 Identify tangible and intangible *value drivers* in the business model.
3 Get early customers/adopters used to *understanding* the worth of the uniqueness or newness and to *accepting* initial pricing levels.
4 *Do not compromise* on pricing right away, as it destroy confidence in the newness and uniqueness of the innovation.
5 *Work collaboratively* to develop value and pricing programs (innovation, product development, pricing, technology, sales).
6 Focus on important *value messages* based on value proposition and critical value drivers → educate users.

Figure 10.7. Recommendations for the early stages of the product life cycle.

Defending your prices means defending your value

One caveat is to maintain your price integrity. This is vitally important. The temptation is strong to use price as a lever to make a sale, especially if you have fallen behind on some of your financial targets. Don't do it! The damage is not only immediate but lasting. You destroy the confidence in the newness and uniqueness of the innovation, but more importantly, you destroy confidence in your organization. How credible will your stories be in the future, and how firm will your resulting prices points be, if you give ground so easily right after launch? I know from experience that it is very hard and requires a lot of discipline for organizations to stand their ground. Don't make this compromise right away, and only make it—if at all—when the decision is unavoidable and essentially makes itself for you. These risks are serious, but I poke some fun at them in the comic in figure 10.8.

Value-based marketing: Testing your storytelling skills

Doing this work in the early stages after product launch marks your transition to the second of the three value-driven strategies

Figure 10.8. Forget the tricks. Focus on value and hold your ground.

you can pursue: value-based marketing. The guidelines we will go into now apply not only to new products but to established products as well. Central to value-based marketing are your customer success stories. These stories don't tell themselves, and they are not effective unless they are polished and shared. Someone needs to stay in contact with your customers, document the value successes they have, prepare the stories through the right media—videos, blogs, speaking engagements, other forms of testimonials—and use your communications channels to make sure these stories find a wide audience. Because we are talking about dollarized value propositions, you should supplement the presumably qualitative stories from your customers with as much quantitative information as possible, either from them or from your own data. You should also work with opinion leaders and create an arsenal of value-selling materials.

This approach is much different from what companies traditionally do, which is to send out product data sheets and maybe a segment brochure. These are fixed forms of communication based on what you think internally. The improvement comes when you flip this dynamic around and let the external information drive your marketing efforts and sales efforts. I show this progression in figure 10.9.

Following these steps yields a whole new set of marketing tools which have both quantitative and qualitative aspects. You can pair up the customer success stories with your own internal ones about how you used a VBP approach to develop and price the product. The business world has an appetite for best practices and stories giving an inside look at the processes that successful companies follow. This can enhance your company's reputation and help cement confidence in the customer value you claim. These tools

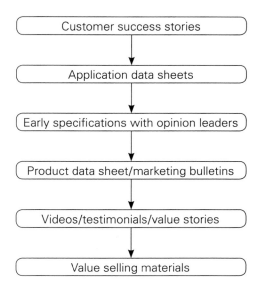

Figure 10.9. The steps to value-based marketing, which is driven by external input (customer stories, opinion leaders, etc.)

can also be very tactical, saving the reader some time. There is no reason why you can't call out your points of differentiation, one by one, to make them explicit in one sheet. Then you can express these benefits in dollars, over the short, medium, and long term. Depending on how you phrase the questions, FAQs are also an effective method. They demonstrate that you know your audience well enough to anticipate and address their concerns. You will find a longer list of these tools in figure 10.10. Over time and through my many projects, I have listed over 55 value-based marketing tools that are being used by the value master companies around the world. Not all of them will be relevant to every company, and their usage varies by industry and customer segment. The point I am trying to make here is that it is time for industrial firms to move from traditional B2B marketing to a more value-based marketing approach that focuses on customer value, access to the value chain, and value communication.

None of this matters unless you share it, not only with your potential customers and other external communication targets but also internally with sales. When a salesforce doesn't do something, the problem is usually not a lack of desire. It is a lack of

Top 10 value-based marketing tools:
1 External customer value success stories
2 Internal success stories with value and price
3 Value bulletins
4 Customer value files
5 Account value scorecard
6 Value calculators (TCO, dollarization, savings)
7 Key differentiation message sheet
8 Dollarized value propositions
9 Application data sheets with ROI/TCO/value
10 Value and differentiation FAQs

Figure 10.10. In my experience, these are the top value-based marketing tools.

MARKETING IS THE R&D OF SALES.

useful information and tools. Huge binders with research reports and spreadsheets are not useful tools for sales. They need communications material and messages in a form that gets them excited and makes them eager to build that information into their own selling strategies. You could basically say that marketing is creating a product of its own, one that needs to recognize the needs of its customers (sales) and then provides the right benefits in a compelling way. Marketing is the R&D of sales. Their products are customer knowledge and value communication tools and messages.

If only it were as easy as I've just described it. The relationship between sales and marketing is an uneasy one in many organizations. Sales claims they do not get enough support from marketing, which often has an attitude and looks down on them. Marketing sees sales as self-interested, pushy, overconfident, and unwilling to listen. While there will always be some people who fit these stereotypes, I know from working intensively with both sides that these views are exaggerated and that there is potential for very beneficial cooperation if each side lets down its guard. And in this case, I think marketing would be well advised to make the first step and fulfill its role as the R&D of sales. Marketing has to step up its efforts and equip the sales team with the right tools in front of the almighty B2B buyers. You are all on the same team, and an openness to new ideas can break down many barriers, which can be high, as I show in figure 10.11.

Now, I must give you a word of caution here regarding your value-based marketing programs. You do need to get the legal team on board to ensure that all your differentiation claims and value stories can be sustained in front of your customers. In many instances, the legal department will not bless the use of dollarized value numbers with customers, at least in writing. They will recommend softer value claims or savings ranges. They might also insist that you include long disclaimers in value bulletins or customer success stories. In some countries, it is flat out illegal to compare your performance to that of other manufacturers. In

Figure 10.11. Marketing should "tear down this wall"...or at least open the gate.

these situations, think of it as the reality of doing business. Do not fight this battle. In the end, it is what it is. Work within the legal and resource constraints and accomplish whatever you can within them. In my experience, there are two kinds of legal teams: facilitators and blockers. The facilitators will say "let's try to find the best way to do that within the law" and the blockers will simply say "no, you can't do that." This is also a reality you have to accept.

The last of the three value-based strategies is value-based selling. Sales can work wonders if they have the right tools, especially credible dollarized value propositions, and the right level of confidence. They need the customer success stories, which accentuate the positive, but they also need support to meet and counter buyers' objections with the appropriate value responses. This requires training on multiple fronts. It means training on the VBP concepts and the link between differentiation and customer value. It also means training, perhaps in the form of mock negotiations, on the preparation of customized value stories and the best ways to handle customer objections.

Value-based selling represents a whole new set of tools for handling the differentiation objections and the price objectives that a sales team might face. They need the conviction and confidence to use case studies to get people on board with value scripts and value selling guides. It involves much more than pricing, as you see in figure 10.12.

Value-based selling: Going from feature-based discussions to value-based discussions

Anyone can do an EVE. What do you do with it to make it work for you? In the end it becomes a communication story. Crafting the stories, telling them well, and living them day to day requires the

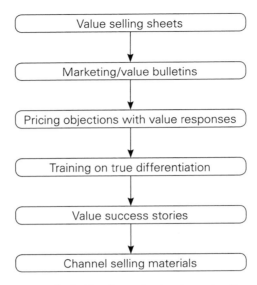

Figure 10.12. The flow of value-based selling.

proper mindset. How do you communicate value with confidence and consistency and engage the customer in value conversations? You use clear messages tailored to the customers' language. The simpler these messages are, the better it is for sales (which needs to absorb and internalize them) and for customers (who need to get excited and appreciate and understand the hard facts).

This is the discipline of value communication. You need the internal and external corporate communications teams involved. You need campaigns around the value stories and drivers, and not around product features. You need to align the communication strategies with the value strategies. This may be a significant change for sales teams, which used to hold discussions driven by product features and may have focused too much on price at the expense of selling value first.

This mindset may take some time to change. Traditionally you use techniques to get mindsets to change, such as motivation or

changing the language. You have carrots and sticks, which means you can use everything from praise and perks to financial incentives; any of these may prove effective. There's no need to go wild unless you have exhausted traditional approaches to mindset change. Don't expect people to just "do things." Goals and incentives are at the heart of any major corporate transformation (see figure 10.13). You need to make sure that the incentives are logical and meaningful, which means they are aligned with overall goals and supportive of them. Mindset is everything!

Mindset is no more than setting the actions and attitude. You need the right mindset if sales, who owns the most customer touchpoints, is to build that final stable bridge between value creation and value capture. When you start thinking of mindset as a business program that transforms the way you go to market, that link is clear.

Tying it all together: You need to develop a culture of value

The work you have done on VBP gives you the basis for developing a culture of value. The greater the collaboration between teams, the higher the level of pricing adoption you will see. You cannot do it without a great level of collaboration in your culture. You

Figure 10.13. Get your goals and incentives right if you want to change a mindset.

need confidence and capabilities, but collaboration is also key. The essence of the homework is in cross-functional communication. People work together, get to know each other, understand common customer needs, define them, keep each other honest, and dollarize the value they collectively see.

People will not necessarily break down their silos or fortresses and do this on their own. It helps to appoint a champion who can catalyze things. This is a special role. You need a bridge builder with real customer experience who can handle quantitative and qualitative discussions with equal skill. These people may be hard to find, and don't expect your team members to line up outside your door.

But the impact is clear. A study by the Professional Pricing Society in April 2011 showed that the behavior of an internal pricing champion—which I would rename a value champion—had a positive and significant impact on a firm's relative performance, capabilities, and organizational confidence. This confidence in turn spread to other parts of the firm.

The secret sauce is that there is nothing in this book you cannot do. With the right effort and commitment and the discipline to follow the guidance, you can do all of this! But you have to combine tangible and intangible elements, and you cannot neglect the emotional and subjective side as you infiltrate, grow your base, and permeate the company. You also need to meet the prerequisites we talked about earlier, such as clear, unequivocal top-down support. Figure 10.14 shows what a culture of value entails. This is the difference between the value masters and the value managers. Value masters recognize intuitively that value is in every process, and that not all of it is visible or tapped yet.

The changes mean that routines, habits, and frames of reference will change. The value champion needs someone who is responsible for keeping people accountable and knowing they are doing the work. The champion is the evangelist, the visionary, the change agent, and the diplomat, but someone needs to make sure people stay on the path. Mindset is everything.

How do you start down this path?

How do you get started? If you start with EVE, you need a lot of training up front (see figure 10.15). When I mentioned the myths around VBP earlier, I said that VBP is not a training program. That is true. But that doesn't mean that VBP requires no training. You can't absorb these ideas instantly through osmosis. When starting VBP projects, I often find big differences in perceptions, conceptualization, and experience among the various players in the project. You do need to spend time bringing everyone onto the

- CEO championing
- Organizational design
- Goals and incentives
- Cross-function collaboration
- Customer orientation
- Long-term orientation/resilience
- Discipline of execution
- Value mindset and behaviors
- Change management and leadership
- Transformational learning

Figure 10.14. A culture of value: What does that entail?

same page. Doing basic training in multifunctional teams helps with this. Setting up a value or pricing council also helps to align knowledge, attention, and desire. You can also conduct a VBP readiness assessment to discover the overall level of maturity.

If you need to infiltrate, the innovation process is the best place to start showing people the value of conducting EVEs. Integrate

How do you get started?
1 Train, *train*, train on value, value-based pricing and EVE.
2 Integrate EVE into your *innovation* process.
3 *Pilot* EVE and value-based strategies with your differentiated products, services, and solutions.
4 Demonstrate success and *impact* of pilot programs.
5 Conduct *second pilot* programs of full value strategies.
6 Hold value *workshops* with innovation, marketing, and sales teams.
7 Slowly *proliferate* value-based strategies to the core business.
8 Measure, measure, *measure* the success of your process.

Figure 10.15. Ways to get started down the path to value-based pricing and a value-based culture.

there, and at the same time look for pilot programs with your existing differentiated products, services, and solutions. I emphasize the word *pilot* here because you need your own success stories to develop the goodwill that will unlock additional resources and create an appetite for more value-based work. This transition will never happen overnight.

Measuring what you do is the step that keeps the loop going. Evidence and validation build confidence, and a dollarized value proposition is by definition measurable. Create facts, create success stories, proliferate them to the core business, and measure success with a corporate tracker of value.

Some things to keep in mind

1 **Consider your VBP project to be a business or go-to-market program.** Bring the right team on board right away across the four pillars: innovation, marketing, pricing, and sales.
2 **Remember that "culture eats strategy for breakfast," as Peter Drucker would remind us.** As you design your VBP project, also evaluate where your culture might

not support the project. Address the potential barriers and resistance as part of the project, using change management methodologies.

3 **Marketing must drive.** Although pricing teams often begin VBP projects, marketing teams need to lead the charge, especially in the areas of segmentation, differentiation value analysis, and value communication. Without their support, their resources, and their help in getting the relevant value data, your project might be derailed or get isolated.

4 **Do not forget internal functions that can support your VBP project.** The HR team can help with internal communication and with developing training roadmaps. Your communications team can help craft professional value stories. Your technical support team can help communicate value messages to a different audience. Your customer service teams can spread the value message every day. All on board!

5 **Do not try to boil the ocean right off the bat.** Think of VBP as an incremental deployment process that requires cross-functional collaboration, change management, and top champions leading the charge. Control the pace and the intensity of the execution to make sure confidence grows slowly but surely.

11

Operationalizing Value-Based Pricing to Enable Salesforce Effectiveness

IN THE PREVIOUS CHAPTER, *I mentioned value-based selling as one of the core applications—beyond pricing—of what you discovered and documented as you progressed through the value-based pricing (VBP) process. Value-based selling deserves some elaboration. It is the last frontier and the place where the rubber meets the road. Many initiatives fail because of breakdowns and lack of execution skills in sales, amplified by the lack of training in strategic negotiation. Breakdowns usually relate to misaligned compensation structures, lack of leadership courage, weak differentiation versus competition, inadequate training programs, and so forth.*

I don't blame the salesforce for this situation, a point I have repeated since the beginning of this book. Turning this around and preventing future breakdowns is less about talent and more about structured preparation, including a solid foundation in listening and storytelling skills. Keys to success in value-based selling include thorough documentation, practice and training on overcoming a buyer's objections, and monitoring and validating the value you deliver.

When firms have limited differentiation in the marketplace and lack a compelling customer value proposition, chances are they will face competitive pressures, experience high discounting levels, and face price wars. But should this happen to companies that have meaningful, measurable differentiation and a compelling customer value proposition? I argue that it shouldn't, and the leaders in companies that understand their value agree. These leaders realize that aggressive discounting behaviors are no longer tolerable, and they want to change the selling behaviors of their sales representatives.

The problem is that many of these leaders also think that training works like a magic spell. Retreat into the world of some marketing wizard for a couple of days, and voilà: the salespeople are value sellers, ready to change the organization's fortunes! This idea is a bit far-fetched. A two-day training session will not address the root cause of their value and pricing problems. These leaders also validate Albert Einstein's purported definition of insanity: keep training your salesforce on negotiation every year and thinking that a different outcome is going to miraculously happen. Sales-force for value is necessary, but two other things have to happen for VBP to take hold. The first is an upstream commitment to innovation and marketing that will reinforce and establish greater differentiation. No amount of training or sales skills in the world can offset a product problem stemming from a lack of differentiation. Second is a commitment to making value-based selling a day-to-day activity. The sales team must live and breathe the value propositions and have access to selling tools based on its core components. They need to take concrete actions to understand value, dollarize value, and engage customers in value conversations.

Those give you the ingredients for a strong sales story (see figure 11.1). As I have said before, your value story and your dollarized differentiation won't sell themselves. Customer value

Figure 11.1. If you want to counter demands for a greater discount, start with a better story.

won't get captured on its own any more than pricing power will suddenly appear in your ERP! It needs advocates telling the right story in front of the customer, not the kinds of storytelling you see in the comic above. Let's start with the importance of preparation as a way to counter and overcome the buyers' tactics.

Combating the buyers' tactics: Win before you begin

"Combat" may be a strong word to describe a sales negotiation. But the similarities to combat, sports, and games become clear when you consider that negotiation involves two opposing parties using available strategies and tactics to win or to gain the upper hand. The following quote from Sun Tzu's *The Art of War* describes the situation quite accurately: "Hence to fight and conquer in all your battles is not supreme excellence; supreme excellence consists in breaking the enemy's resistance without fighting."

In other words, you win before the battle begins. Selling on value—and negotiating to capture it—requires preparation, chess-playing skills, and a capacity to outmaneuver the other side. It requires the kind of playbook (see figure 11.2) that allows the sales team to quantify and practice the most likely "what if?" situations they could face. None of the tricks, traps, and standard

Negotiation is a game. Design your own playbook.
- Anticipate tricks and traps and get ready for them.
- Be ready for standard pricing objections.
- Be ready for contentious discussions on value estimation level.
- Prepare your options, scenarios, bargaining zone.
- Be ready to politely walk away or ask for more time.
- If you need to blow off steam, ask for a break.

Figure 11.2. The negotiation playbook is not theoretical but is rather a real-world compilation of what a salesperson needs in order to respond confidently and appropriately.

objections I cite in this chapter should be complete news to experienced salespeople. What is new here is that they have predetermined ways to see through the tricks, avoid the traps, and respond confidently to the standard objections. The advance preparation and practice help take the emotion out of the sales negotiation and keep the basis level-headed and rational.

In my experience, many salespeople do not take the time to prepare thoroughly for customer visits, for value conversations, for tough negotiations, or for new situations. Introducing value-based prices, complete with the new value propositions and the dollarized facts to back them up, is a new situation for them. Some tool and tricks in their current toolbox will still be valuable. You are not starting from scratch. But even these tools may require adjustment and refinement. Better to do that beforehand, such as in a mock negotiation with a trainer with your colleagues, than on the fly in front of the buyers. Value selling and value management are no place for improvisation. The salespeople need to know their walk-away prices and thresholds, and if there is any uncertainty, they need to ask and clear them up with their leadership. They need to know the incumbent currently selling to those customers, their differentiation position, and the dollarized value they might bring to customers versus that incumbent. That requires much more value discovery up front and better preparation.

Just as customers fall into different segments based on their needs and willingness-to-pay, we can also segment buyers according to their attitudes. The largest groupings would be value partners, poker players, and price buyers. A proper value-messaging strategy requires a clear understanding of the buying dynamics on the other side, and your value messages will need to vary based on the nature and power of the various stakeholders in the decision-making process. Value buyers tend to seek a longer-term win for both parties, but that doesn't mean you can let your guard down. You still need to make sure you beat your competitors with the best possible value stories.

Poker players and price buyers are more likely to play games, including spreading misinformation and restricting your access to other members of the organization. If they become territorial and stonewall you, you should still try to make contact whenever possible with other departments at the customer location. One way around them is to visit trade shows and make contacts there with marketing or management professionals. Attending industry association meetings is also a good way to diversify your interactions with your customers. These positive exposures to your value stories can help exert a pull effect on buyers who are otherwise resistant to any push efforts from your side.

Some companies do not allow their salesforce to attend industry events or trade shows. That is a shame. They may be missing an opportunity to deliver critical value messages, discuss value savings estimations, and test the value of potential new offerings with people who actually use and apply your products rather than the people tasked with procuring them.

Another way to break the procurement department's stranglehold on the value selling process is to separate the transactional process from the relational process. Many organizations have already done this, designing their salesforce structure so that marketing, application development, and business development professionals focus exclusively on the relational selling process. They devote their time to value messaging, value selling, getting their products or services spec'ed, and collecting value-in-use data. They leave the "dirty work" to the transactional salesforce, whose strengths lie in tactical negotiations, order taking, and forecasting. The two teams work hand in hand to achieve the optimal combined outcome: value selling and negotiation for value. Each knows its exact roles and responsibilities, and clear standard operating procedures limit the chances of overlap.

Stakeholder analysis is an important part of your planning. You are dealing with living, breathing human beings, not just boxes and names on an org chart. Value selling requires the use of different value messages for each stakeholder in the decision-making process. Salespeople need to fully grasp the influence and power in the buying center and the roles of all stakeholders. It is essential that you be able to answer these questions ahead of any negotiation:

- Who holds the final decision-making power?
- Who gets involved in the decision-making process?
- What external parties can make the transaction easier?
- What value messages are critical for each internal stakeholder?

The bottom line is that you sell, promote, and message on value differently in front of each stakeholder. Each requires special attention and different preparation. Different actors will react to different value messages. The art of value selling is tailoring the messages to whoever is in front of you during the transactional or relational selling process. Adopting a one-message-fits-all approach is not the most appropriate one, as some messages will not resonate with the audience you are facing. As your relationships with other actors in the decision-making process get stronger, the transactional relationship with the buyers will also improve.

Less marketing and more storytelling: Leveraging your documentation

You have read several times in this book that documentation is critical for preparation. A powerful and dynamic reservoir of this documentation is the customer value file (CVF). Another is value scorecards. The CVF is not a notepad where you can jot down fluffy or nice-to-have things. It is the arsenal of hard facts (and the evidence that supports them) and the value stories you need for support in your value-selling efforts at a specific customer. These are the arguments you will need when you face rational or sophisticated buyers, and they will give you the chips to counter with when your salesforce sits down at the table with the poker players. You'll find the characteristics of a superior CVF in figure 11.3.

The information collected in the CVF is the basis for your storytelling efforts at that customer, so you have to make sure the CVF is well stocked and up to date. I elaborate on the storytelling aspects after reviewing what each of these factors in figure 11.3 means.

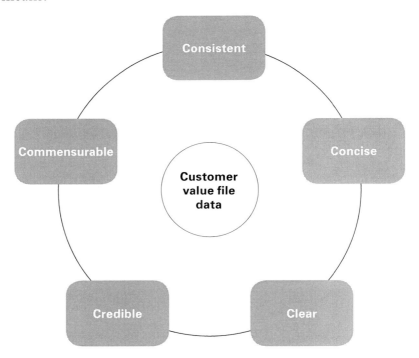

Figure 11.3. A superior, reliable customer value file meets some strict requirements.

- **Commensurable.** This is the number one factor! Value is a number, so you have to be able to quantify all value drivers using relevant data and logical, applicable formulas. When you keep the buyers focused on quantified and attractive savings or upside, you have a much better chance of deflecting their pricing objections.

- **Credible.** Buyers will challenge your math and your data, especially if the approach you take is new or makes them uncomfortable. The CVF should enable you to show your work, so to speak, so that the buyers see the full derivation. Transparency and openness on the data, the math, and the repeatability of the work helps build trust. In some cases you can even show where you scaled back a case to a more realistic number, in order to establish credibility.

- **Consistent.** VBP was an education process for your organization, so you can imagine how the buyers feel when you come with a new pricing regime. You have to present your data in a consistent manner quarter after quarter, because this is an education process for the buyers, too. The repetition and reinforcement helps establish the language and the math of value in their minds and their organizations as well.

- **Concise.** In my experience it is hard for a company to focus on more than five critical value drivers. As you read earlier, I insist on a maximum of three drivers when I work closely with an organization. Having too many value drivers diverts attention and waters down the value story. Once you have this core created, you could add some sections on some softer, nice-to-have drivers, but don't let this distract from the overall focus.

- **Clear.** Use direct language. George Orwell once recommended never using a long word where a short, simple one will do. You need to build your CVF with customer needs, perceived benefits, and the customer's own vocabulary in mind. Words have to resonate with buyers and have to reflect costs savings or incremental revenues in their operations. Put yourself in the customer's shoes when you build your models and create your stories.

Leveraging your CVF in your negotiations with a buyer is at the heart of the value-selling process, but it requires special story-telling skills. You can't simply read off data points or recite value messages one after the other. Sales representatives and account managers should learn how to develop a CVF, and then practice, in groups, using the CVF to deliver impactful responses to pricing objections. They should receive storytelling training and learn how to deliver a credible value story to buyers. The winning recipe for those stories is a combination of the facts in the CVF and the style of the specific buyer. Recognizing those styles and crafting the appropriate stories requires training and experience.

Handling customer pricing objections

The nature and intensity of the pricing objections will depend on whether the sellers face a value buyer, a poker player, or a pure price buyer. Figure 11.4 shows some of the most common

> The typical pricing objections
> - "Your price is too high."
> - "It is not within the budget guidelines."
> - "Your competition offered us a better deal."
> - "I must put this out for bid."
> - "That is more than I want to spend."
> - "This is outside the guidelines I received for this category."
> - "I can make a quick call and get it for a lot less."
> - "You are really outside the ballpark number."

Figure 11.4. I'm sure these objections are familiar to you. Do you have a way to counter each one?

objections the purchasing team will bring up. The pure price buyers will use these passionately and try to make them the main focus of the negotiation.

Overcoming these objections is almost impossible without preparation, but even that is not everything. Perhaps the most underrated skill, and one in demand in the heat of the negotiation itself, is listening. When the salesforce has the keen ability to listen, it creates an opportunity to build empathy, to know when a certain value message is not getting through, and to recognize when the negotiating partner—particularly the poker player—is not only objecting but setting a trap as well. Before we get to listening, though, let's take another look at preparation. You have to study your playbook (see figure 11.2) and know it inside and out.

Study the playbook. The best way to study the playbook and internalize it is to make the effort a group rather than an individual one. Any salesperson *individually* will have a few objections or types of buyers that he or she knows very well, but *collectively* the salesforce has a wide and deep range of experience with nearly all common objections and buyers. Getting the salesforce together in a room to review all standard price objections is a good exercise. They can vent and release their stress out in the open among peers. Once they have reviewed the standard objections, they can tap into their actual experiences to come up with basic solutions and responses. The final step is to bring in someone from the marketing communications team to package these as a playbook.

The playbook can also serve as a useful training tool for new sales representatives. Sales will be more inclined to accept the playbook and depend on it because they themselves are the source of the information. This is a much more credible approach than if marketing developed the playbook and "threw it over the wall" to sales.

Figure 11.5 offers some high-level tips for handling price objections. The first is to divorce yourself from the process and to not take objections personally. We all know that negotiating for value can challenge the self-esteem of even your best sales representatives. They have to keep their emotions and egos in check. Price objections are part of the process, and few things the buyers do should catch your salespeople by surprise. Any negotiation that does not include price objections might mean that the buyer is not serious about transacting with you.

Listen! Excellence at value selling means taking control of the conversation, of the surrounding space, and of time. It requires superior listening skills at all levels. The unfortunate reality is that few people listen well enough, from leaders and managers to salespeople and their counterparts on the other side of the table. This may have biological roots. Telling our stories is a positive experience, and our good feelings can diminish our ability to properly observe the audience, gauge their reactions, and make adjustments. When we fail to do these things, we miss opportunities to probe, and we miss valuable information.

Telling a convincing story does not mean delivering a robotic monologue or a data dump. It is an interactive dialogue. Careful and purposeful listening allows the salesperson to ask open-ended

Tips to handle pricing objections
- Divorce your ego from the sale: don't be defensive, and don't argue.
- Create a pricing objection file with standard value responses, customer past behaviors, and tips to build your confidence.
- Anticipate objections in a positive way. It is part of the job.
- Help the buyer save face: recap, repharse, respect, reward the buyer.
- Listen with all senses: words, body language, emotions, mood.

Figure 11.5. Handling price objections.

follow-up questions (*"why is that?"* or *"tell me more about that!"*) and to send and receive unspoken signals and clues. They should nod and take notes to convey genuine interest. They should maintain eye contact and watch the buyer's body language. Pauses in a conversation are natural, and salespeople should use this time to reflect and avoid jumping to quick conclusions or giving knee-jerk responses. I follow the two-second rule before answering a question to make sure I have understood the question or comment properly.

The best acts of value selling are value conversations, and these focus on issues that can make the dialogue between buyer and seller "professionally personal." Here are some questions a salesperson can ask to spark a fruitful value conversation:

- *What keeps you up at night?*
- *How can I help you be more successful?*
- *What prevents you from being more successful?*
- *How do you beat your competition day-in and day-out?*
- *How do you define success in your world?*

The more you engage the buyer in a conversation, the more success you will have.

Identify and avoid the buying traps. Listening is a tough skill to master because you need to listen politely, purposefully, but also critically. Positive emotions can be just as detrimental as negative emotions if they cloud your judgment and leave you open to a trap that a buyer may set. These traps fall into a few broad categories.

- **Exaggerated claims.** Buyers may overstate the urgency or inflate the risk if you don't reach a deal ("all your business is at stake" or "no second chances"). Each is potentially a trap to make you sweat and force a quick concession.

- **Misinformation.** They may question your quality. They may misrepresent how much the competition has charged or is bidding. They may alter the scope or make it ambiguous. Each tactic is designed to diminish your perceived or relative value and thus wring a price concession or a "goodie" from you to enhance the deal.
- **Power plays and scare tactics.** Lack of flexibility is one thing, but some buyers resort to a "my way or the highway" approach, threaten to bring in more people, or issue ultimatums. Such intimidation is designed to force the seller to set any counterarguments aside and concede.
- **Sentimentality or pity.** Buyers may claim that their business is in rough shape and or even in dire straits and needs a lifeline. They may appeal to your friendship or relationship ("we go back years") or portray themselves as the proverbial good cop ("I got this for you, I'm working your interests over here").

Obviously, most of your sales representatives are very experienced and will recognize these based on their knowledge of the account and the buyer's style. The point I am trying to make here is that your organization should have standard value responses to each tactic, and that they should practice their use so that they become second nature.

Defend your credibility. What happens when the customer does not believe your value data? You prepare so intensively in part because you expect this to happen. A buyer who does not believe your value story will have an issue with any perceived differentiation that you offer to him or her. You have a number of qualitative and quantitative arguments to address their concerns. Your first line of defense is rhetorical and focuses primarily on risk and reassurance.

If a loyal customer speaks of switching to a cheaper option, remind them of risks and hidden costs of switching, not just your excellent record. Have stories ready to illustrate what happens in the short and long term when a company sacrifices quality to get a low price. Probe when they say the competitor is cheaper, and have them explain what they are getting for their money (which is less value than what you have offered). Sometimes their argument about a lower price has a very short-term focus, and you can argue that you offer a greater benefit over the product life cycle.

You can openly acknowledge that your prices are higher—if it is clearly no secret—as long as you reinforce your differentiation and do it with pride, confidence, and enthusiasm. Reassure the buyer that they are making the right decision.

If these approaches do not work, you can escalate to more tangible approaches. You can draw on your customer value file (CVF) and review your history in detail, all the while reinforcing your unique selling propositions. If there are no political issues, you can reveal what you have learned from the buyer's colleagues about the value you deliver, and link that to success stories and testimonials from other customers. Finally, you can also offer next steps and terms such as these:

- performance contracts with some risk-sharing mechanisms or penalties
- better or best-in-class warranty
- quarterly reviews to evaluate the incremental savings and performance KPIs
- personal guarantees (if you have built a genuinely strong relationship with the buyer).

To wrap up this chapter, I would like to highlight some additional tools to support your value selling efforts. You will find an overview in figure 11.6.

Your salesforce will have to recognize the type of accounts they are facing and can pull tools out of the toolbox as needed. A value buyer might only need to see a strong CVF. A pure price buyer might require even fewer tools, while a poker player might require more advanced tools to be convinced of your stories.

Value documentation. This extends beyond the CVF. Quantified case studies and user testimonials are also very powerful. An often overlooked but important source of documentation is customer service and technical service reports, which not only prove out your quality but also show the number of touch points you have with the customer. Select the best and most relevant documents, but don't overwhelm the buyer.

Value reminders. These are more tactical and might not involve the buyers. You can address them to your customers' R&D

❶ Value documentation:
- No charge invoice
- Customer value file
- Project savings report
- Warranty reports
- Quantified case studies
- Customer service action reports
- User testimonials
- Contract anniversary with value data

❷ Value reminders
- Weekly win reports
- Joint call activities
- Testimonial letters
- Quick win stories

❸ Value audits and meetings
- Formal audits of intended versus delivered value
- Quarterly review of customer value files
- Customer satisfaction surveys
- Supplier performance appraisal

Figure 11.6. Tools for value-selling include documentation, reminders, and monitoring/audits.

departments, supply chain teams, and even your customers' sales-force. The goal is to build or reinforce trust and intimacy with other departments so that you have allies if purchase negotiations get tough. These reminders provide a constant stream of value nuggets!

Value audits and meetings. These powerful tools are more demanding and more formal. They may require some investment on your part. They are traditional tools in the buyer–seller relationship and are most often requested by the buying organization. This is an opportunity to prove and document your value within a framework designed or influenced by the customer. These quarterly value review meetings should be conducted with buyers and also with important stakeholders in the decision-making process. The goal is to validate the value estimates and monitor incremental savings and/or revenues generated by the relationship. These also offer evidence if you have issued a guarantee or made other warranties. I also encourage organizations to use Six Sigma projects in pricing and to design joint team projects to achieve the expected savings. Additional savings may then be shared between the two organizations according to a rule agreed in advance.

Are you ready for value selling?

Best-in-class organizations not only pay special attention to value; they place value at the heart of their organization. That is probably the most overarching prerequisite for successful value selling. If you are serious about value, you should see the need to redirect your selling preparation based on the guidance in this chapter. This includes training programs that encompass customer value propositions, listening skills, handling price objections, presentation skills, and storytelling. Value messaging is part of value selling and is as much art as science. Having said that, the field of value management is no place for improvisation. You can't afford to take value selling lightly, especially after all of the work you have put in so far.

Some things to keep in mind

1 **Value-based selling requires many tools from marketing and more robust preparation from the salesforce.** There is no way around it. B2B buyers are getting more and more sophisticated, and the chances are good that your salesforce is lagging behind.

2 **Everything that is done in a value-based approach and in VBP is intended to better equip the sellers and account managers.** This means that you need to bring them on board early in the process, so that they embrace and assimilate the tools early. They actually need to help design them. The sooner they have skin in the game, the better they can execute the value-based selling approach.

3 **The role of sales is changing in the B2B world.** We are heading toward less transactional selling and more consultative selling. The role of the account manager includes much more than taking orders. They have to help discover customer value, to quantify it for different stakeholders, and to communicate value systematically.

4 **Value-based selling is not the responsibility of the sales team alone.** Marketing, customer service, technical support, customer training, and top management also have to value sell. All must systematically project value messages to the ecosystem in order to win the "messaging war." It is matter of changing customer value perceptions. That takes time, but it is worth the effort.

5 Your salesforce will be bombarded with objections.
They will hear value objections, differentiation objections, needs objections, pricing objections, timing objections, and much more. To help your salesforce combat this barrage of objections, you need to prepare standard responses, rehearse them, and refine them with experience. Selling on value requires practice, courage, and social intelligence. Do not improvise. Get prepared.

12

Putting It All Together: A Value-Based Approach

THE TIME HAS COME *for you to "graduate" from value-based pricing (VBP) and create sustainable capabilities for a competitive advantage. You are ready to disrupt your approach to value management! Several factors contribute to your success as you fully implement VBP and make customer value part of your corporate DNA. One of the most important ones—driven by the communications and sharing models that I have stressed throughout this book—is developing your organizational intelligence. You should also beware of cookie-cutter approaches from consultants. You and your organization need to do this work for yourselves. The unique thing about learning is that you cannot outsource it. You have to do it.*

Customer insights are among the essential fuels that power your VBP efforts. You will need a continuous stream of them across the board if you want to make customer value an integral part of your organization. Putting customers at the center of your activities ("customer centricity") means knowing their ecosystems, understanding their processes in great detail, and speaking the same language. Call it customer centricity or customer intimacy... you cannot succeed at customer value without greater customer orientation.

That statement alone reflects what I have said throughout: VBP is much more than a pricing strategy. It may start that way, but as you lay the foundation and maintain it, the VBP initiative evolves into much more. You are implementing a business strategy and a commercial strategy that touches everything. It is long-term change that makes value the cornerstone and common element of all your business practices.

Pricing is instrumental, but marketing should drive the change. Marketing is the R&D of sales and the lifeblood of strategy, because it is the flow-through point and the processing point for customer insights. You need to connect all parts of the VBP program dynamically in a way that leads to a synchronized flow of insights. That means that you don't take an approach with several speeds. The entire organization works together at the same speed with the same content, in order to get a stable flow. This will necessitate a change in behavior. And the nature and pace of the change is important. You should embrace incremental change. I never recommend brutal, disruptive change to pricing unless the business is in dire trouble.

Theory versus reality: It's time for you to act

No matter what you've measured or estimated, your differentiation exists only in theory unless you can execute on it. This is when you find out whether your differentiation is real. If you have quality issues with your products or services, if you can't deliver on time, or if your people are unfriendly, the best-intended models in the world won't save you. If your business model is broken and you have waited too long to innovate, you may have passed the tipping point. To compensate for these shortcomings, customers will place you in the commodity category and will ask for discounts. They will want to know how much you will compensate them for your deficits, such as bad delivery. From their perspective, this fits with the logic of the value pool. If the real value you deliver is lower than you planned, you cannot justify the same prices. You need performance and execution, not just paper value.

I have offered guidance in every chapter of this book, but I do not claim to have a rigid, cookie-cutter approach. No two companies I have ever worked with are identical enough to be able to carbon copy an approach from someone else and make it their own. Standard approaches, however, are the bread-and-butter of consultants, which means you should beware. You need long-term skills from people who care. Keep in mind that a consultant will not do the real work for you. You don't need consultants. You need coaches. Do your own work!

The three primary reasons for this are uniqueness, independence, and power. As I mentioned above, your company differs from every other company in its history, talent, strategy, reputation, assets, and scale. The differences may be slight in each case, but cumulatively these place you in a unique position, even if you are competing in a market that others (not me!) would describe as highly commoditized. So any standard approach that seems attractive will require considerable customization. It requires work.

Second, by doing your own work you achieve independence and continuity. You develop a new "your way" that does not depend on the ongoing presence of expensive consultants and that can be transferred to new employees with relative ease. Finally, doing the work on your own brings power. It can turn into a serious competitive advantage, in part because it makes you more nimble, it makes you more knowledgeable, and it increases your pricing power. You have to treat learning as something with that kind of potential. That means you provide the skills development, so that your current and future teams can do VBP in a repetitive, scalable manner. You need to build organizational intelligence for the long term. You can't outsource learning. Peter Senge, an MIT systems scientist and the author of the classic book *The Fifth Discipline,* writes, "In the long run, the only sustainable advantage is your organization's ability to learn faster than the competition."

Who is successful at organizational learning and staying consistently ahead of the competition? You would expect such companies to be synonymous with innovation and value, to have both diversity and focus, and to be recognized as leaders in their market because of actual leadership and not merely because they have the highest market share. Those are appropriate ways to describe the companies you see in figure 12.1. These companies have value ingrained in their processes. It is not something tangential to their success or a byproduct of it. It is their secret sauce.

These companies have realized that value doesn't happen by accident and that sustaining it requires training, processes, commitment, and effort. They have built their own capabilities. This allows them to create value, measure it systematically, and capture it with the right sharing mechanisms, because they are keenly aware of the value they generate. It is a wheel that turns. These are

Figure 12.1. What do these companies have in common? They are value masters: they have value ingrained in their organizations.

the companies that sustain a value process over time and become value masters.

Saying it is a wheel that turns may sound like a cliché, but the value masters really do ignite a virtuous cycle that turns value into money and then back into more value. The process begins with strategic innovation. Careful and constant study and customer intimacy have enabled them to identify the gaps and needs in their markets and segments and to decide which ones to address. This leads to value creation with a focus on clear and measurable differentiation. When it comes to the critical three to five drivers, the value masters deal only in superlatives. It's about "better" and "best" versus the competition. "Good" or "good enough" creates no differentiated value for the customer. Value masters make value assessments and dollarize their differentiation, so that they can build the fact-based stories that establish and sell their value, and so that they know how large their value pool is. Then they capture that value through VBP, and reinvest the profits to continue the cycle. Figure 12.2 illustrates this cycle.

What is very interesting about figure 12.2 is that VBP is only one of the five stops in the cycle. This cycle is a management story, not a pricing story. VBP is an essential part of something larger: a value-based culture. You can see in each phase, including VBP, how this cycle weaves together the core business functions of value-based innovation, marketing, pricing, and selling with the three steps of value: creation, communication, and capture. Such a culture can survive and thrive only when you have fluid communication and collaboration that breaks down the silos. You train together, not by function, and you trust in the abilities of your colleagues.

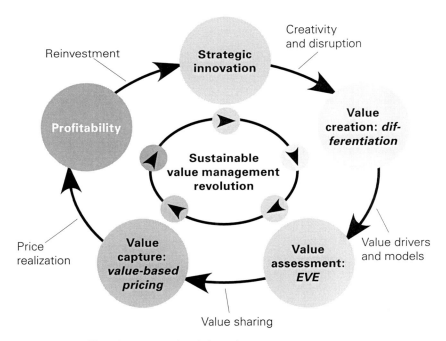

Figure 12.2. The virtuous cycle of the value masters.

Belief in the virtuous cycle in figure 12.2 on its own is not sufficient to make it work. The value masters have a mix of talent and capabilities that ensures that they meet the demands of each part of the cycle. I summarize these capabilities in figure 12.3 and will highlight some of them. These are the characteristics that make value masters different from other organizations.

Engineering talent. Building the bridge from feature to benefit to dollarization requires an ability to make comparisons with the products and services your competitors offer, as well as the ability to replicate processes your customers have, so that you can understand them better. Independent third-party information will provide some credibility, but you have to have the in-house capability to understand and interpret this information, do your own testing, and make complex assessments on your own. Your team should be able to understand what aspects you need to take into account when you measure total cost of ownership (TCO) and

Capabilities of best-in-class value masters:
- *Application engineers*: TCO, value-in-use, and techno-marketing.
- A robust user-need *segmentation process*: based on qualitative, quantitative, and data-driven analytics.
- A powerful *upfront* customer *value discovery process*.
- *VOC and market knowledge*: systematic, consistent, and rich.
- *Proprietary* value quantification *tools*: ROI calculators, TCO, value databases.
- *Relational vs. transactional selling*: separate organizations with common goals and compensation systems.
- *Advanced training programs*: value, differentiation, pricing, negotiation, etc.
- *Deep knowledge of competitors*: collection, treatment, modeling.
- *Internal technical/engineering centers*: data warehouses and banks.
- *CRM systems* that collect and connect all relevant data.

Figure 12.3. What makes value masters different from other companies.

value in use. An organization that learns and applies the learnings will also have internal technical and engineering centers, where they can warehouse data, findings, and insights.

Marketing skills. You know by now that these two words mean something specific and special in terms of VBP. When I say that you need to know your competitors and customers better than they know themselves, who will do that, what process do they follow, and what are their goals? Voice-of-customer and value-discovery processes are two important components. Listening to your customers, knowing how they themselves create value, and looking for ways to improve their internal processes, save them money, grow their business, and enhance their confidence require a permanent and intense closeness.

Tools and systems. I include segmentation here as well, even though it is driven by customer and market knowledge, to emphasize that it is a formal process, not an ad hoc exercise. Beyond that, you need your own proprietary tools for quantifying value, ROI, and TCO and for storing your data in an accessible, transferable way. You need to have a CRM system that serves as the glue that collects and connects all relevant data. Finally, you need to have advanced training programs to ensure that your teams have a level of proficiency and a shared vocabulary for value, differentiation, marketing, pricing, and negotiation.

I could add commitment to this list. When the value masters need to make decisions, their teams do not need to resist the temptations you see in the comic in figure 12.4. The direction in which they are headed is clear. The value masters represent the gold standard that I would love you to attain. But this is a journey, and in your current state you will probably be quite a distance from this

Figure 12.4. Pursuing value means breaking habits and avoiding the easy way out.

standard. How do you get your change process started, and how do you know how well you are doing?

The change in your internal mindset should lead you away from short-term gratification and quick fixes. Your change management program should be subject to many of the same rules that apply to a value culture itself: measurement, transparency, simplicity, and flexibility. You need to establish and track a series of change management KPIs to see how often and how effectively the tools are being used and how well you are achieving your objectives. How many EVEs have you completed? How many people have you trained? How many new value propositions have you created? You will find an overview of these KPIs in figure 12.5.

The financial KPIs top the list because ultimately these are the metrics whose potential you are trying to unlock and fulfill. Money makes the wheel in figure 12.2 spin steadier and faster.

Financial KPIs:
- Gross margin (current vs. budget vs. previous year)
- Average sales price (current vs. budget vs. previous year)
- Average discounts (current vs. budget vs. previous year)

Change management KPIs:
- % of adoption of change
- Proficiency level (survey and assessment)
- Utilization rate of new tools or methods

Value KPIs (qualitative):
- % of target population trained on value
- # of created and published customer value propositions
- Value culture index quarterly score
- % of time spent with customer on value activities
- Utilization rate of value tools

Figure 12.5. Tracking value on a dashboard through KPIs.

Improved margins, the "right" selling prices, and a reduction in the level of discount you grant are all pillars of profit improvement. This improvement will be no accident. While it may be hard to show a strict causation between financial performance and any of the change management KPIs and value KPIs, you need some way to track how many people your program has influenced and whether you are producing the right outputs. Tools are only useful if someone uses them. How frequently are your tools being used, and by how many people? How much have your training efforts raised proficiency levels? How much more time are you spending with customers, and at what levels?

The KPIs will help you determine whether your progress has stalled and may help you identify a root cause. One cause may be the size and complexity of the process, so don't try to do too much or aim for a big bang. If your process is too big, people can't keep up. Your process also need to be dynamic, because value itself is dynamic. It is subjective and about perception.

The journey toward VBP probably seemed like a daunting challenge before you picked up this book. Until you become aware of what is truly involved and learn how VBP can provide you with a sustainable and lucrative competitive advantage, it is easy to see VBP as not worth the massive effort. Nonetheless, you may have found parts of the program attractive. A lot of these ideas are in the air when people think about the VBP, but until now, they haven't had a comprehensive resource to fall back on. What was missing from the market was a resource that provides the clear context, makes sense, and builds confidence. This book is a touchstone. As a coach who has worked with large and small B2B companies throughout the world, I aim to provide a standard set of guidance, steps, and definitions that are well articulated and written for everyone in the process.

Remember that, in theory, every company could acquire the tools and resources to launch VBP initiatives. At the same time, remember that fewer than 20 percent of firms use some form of VBP. It is not as easy as it seems. If it were, many more firms would be using it. VBP is about experiential and transformative learning. It is about learning faster and better than your competition. It is not about merely doing customer value analysis or competitive analysis. It is about doing it *better* and in a way that extracts the right insights for the value work. You cannot buy that off the shelves! There is no magic wand. There is teamwork, exploration, and practice. Give it a try. Join the VBP revolution!